REIGN

REIGN

MY STORY AND HOW TO LIVE VICTORIOUSLY OVER SEXUAL IMMORALITY

DAMIEN ELLISON

Heavenly Light Press

Alpharetta, GA

ISBN: 978-1-6653-0286-9 - Paperback
eISBN: 978-1-6653-0287-6 - eBook

Library of Congress Control Number: 2021916960

Published in the United States of America   1 0 0 4 2 1

♾This paper meets the requirements of ANSI/NISO Z39.48-1992 (Permanence of Paper)

Scripture Quotations are from the Comparative Study Bible, Revised Edition Copyright © 1999 by Zondervan

Scripture Quotations BibleApp Daily Study Audio & Prayer, Version 8.26.3 Copyright © 2008-2020 by Life.Church

Cover Art Design: Damascus Media Inc.

Editor: Cara-Marie Findlay

for my firstborn Ledisi Leanne & my children to come,
when temptation arises, may Holy Spirit and the words I
have written in the pages to follow help you live
victoriously over sin.

to my wife, Sectrina, the one I waited for:
thank you for waiting and thank you for standing with me.

CONTENTS

I am still amazed how during my childhood a computer was barely accessible in the home, yet now, the world is at one's fingertips. In this day and age, people can now access information at the rate of only a few seconds. Minds have become accustomed to human approval, thanks to posts, shares, likes, and follows. This hunger for approval drives people to post images of themselves naked or barely clothed, done in an attempt to feel validated by strangers. The images in turn create doors for those viewing them to walk through doors that lead to lust and anything related to sexual immorality. Those of us who look on such things allow so much time to pass us by, lost in a sea of flesh. We lose so much time that could be spent with God, our families, and friends. This could lead us to get sucked into the computer screen and become consumed by sexual immorality instead of living victoriously over it. We don't realize that we were created to *reign* over all things that are sexually immoral.

Our souls search for love and validation from people through social media, the media, careers, and relationships. We're seeking for something meaningful, someone to care for us, someone to love us like no other. We often become impatient and seek solace in the arms of a human being. A human being who cannot love us the way our Creator loves us. A love that has existed before time struck it's first beam of light. One cannot fully comprehend this Love that seeks to love every human. The Love that surpasses human understanding. This love cannot be touched but only believed in. Those who are Saved do dare to imagine or comprehend this love but only to a degree, never fully, while those who are not cannot even begin to imagine. It is the sense of human touch that draws one in, and causes what was, to be lost, if they choose to seek the love of a person first and not God. Lost in a sea of forgetfulness, never remembering what should have been. Forgetting that we are all created to: REIGN.

The need to be loved becomes clouded by how society says one should be loved. The wisdom of man proclaims what humans should live and die for. Wisdom from one's own definition of truth causes many people to live out the lie first told by the serpent who once lived in the heavens. This illegitimate father has made it his eternal mission to throw us off by simply posing a question. That question then leads to reason. Reason turns to compromise. Until compromise finally gives way to action. A fatal decision brought on by one thing. Desire. Wanting whatever we think we want, based on our human nature. You may not even know what you want. Perhaps your curiosity of the unknown may cause desire to give way to action. Ultimately it is desire, wanting something, that leads one person to do right and another person to do wrong.

If we want something we do not have then why do we want it? Curiosity one may say. This is a valid answer. The serpent did a great job in the garden of Eden deceiving Eve into eating the fruit. She did not have the knowledge that came with eating the fruit. The serpent told her a lie, and before you know it, Eve wanted what she was never supposed to have. God may have wanted Adam and Eve to receive the knowledge that came with that fruit, but not until the proper time. Adam and Eve ate the fruit, and obtained that knowledge before the time they were supposed to, and this is what got them in trouble with God.

The same I think can be said when it comes to sexual immorality. Sex was created for marriage. Fornication and other acts of sexual immorality we have done prior to marriage is unacceptable in God's eyes. My own desire to do what is right in God's sight has led me to struggle between my flesh and spirit. On one hand, the man in me wants to have sex and desires a wife, but the spirit in me wants those things the right way, God's way.

You see what many people fail to realize is that sin has one end game: death. It is this (eternal) consequence that has compelled people like myself to accept Christ, and if unwed, to abstain from sex until marriage. I will admit, death can be a scary thing, but it is also a good thing, if you die to the right desires. Death to self, may mean life to your spirit, and life to your spirit may draw many to the Giver of Life.

I have wondered time and time again why God has orchestrated things the way He has. Why has He allowed me to be single for such a long time while my peers enter into the holy covenant called marriage? I now see why I've been single for such a long time: so God can teach me how to Reign Over Sexual Immorality. It is through the pages that follow, that you will see my journey as a single, adult male who has sought to not know a woman sexually until he is married. You will read about my hopes and my dreams of marriage. You will see the disappointments I've endured and the victories I've won. You will also see the temptations I've had to fight through, the call I've had to keep my eyes on; and more importantly the Man I've had to keep my eyes on so that I stay focused on what's important to Him.

My prayer is that the words that follow will strengthen, and encourage, you to follow Christ wholeheartedly; and that they will show you how to Reign Over Sexual Immorality.

CHAPTER ONE

MY JOURNEY

Life took a pivotal turn for me the day before my pastor and his wife got married – Friday, January 11, 2008. I had been asked to be one of the groomsmen, and of course I accepted. However, during the rehearsal for the ceremony, I was informed that the bridesmaid who I was supposed to escort down the aisle would not be able to attend the wedding. I proceeded to walk, with my eyes fixated on the altar, just as nervous as ever. As I approached the altar, I heard these words: "Your journey will be long," the officiant (the lead pastor at my church) declared.

I knew exactly what he meant in that moment. I would be single for a while. What I didn't know at the time, was why. Before I go any further, I want to briefly share why I believe I've been single for quite some time. I always wanted to be married, but those words put me on a quest. A quest into the unknown. My journey as a single man, after those words were spoken, led me to find myself and my calling.

Fast forward through my personal history to July 4, 2015

— Coney Island, New York. My brothers and I had just gotten off the subway, and there were so many people, we could barely move. We had to inch our way through the crowd just to get out of the station. Once out, we continued on to the festivities. I can still remember seeing all the young people in the streets. I wondered what their lives were like. Could it be that all of these young people, in one of the largest cities in the country, did not know Christ? I would love to one day see a live, street-wide concert geared towards preaching Christ to a large number of young people, like the crowd that was gathered before me that day.

Throughout my visit to New York, I wondered where God was. This may sound strange, but after living in Atlanta for many years, New York had a different vibe. The city is filled with people from all walks of life, like any other major city: business professionals, men and women. Brimming with culture. Hip-hop. Full of life and a distinctive way of living. People appear to live tough lives. Lives filled with hard work, pain, disappointments, and triumphs. Going to church, on any given day of the week, is a relief of sorts because those hard-working New Yorkers can seek refuge in the arms of God. They can make their requests known unto Him through prayer and supplication; and make it through each passing day believing that He will one day answer those prayers.

I have sought to live this life believing in the risen Savior. Christ has been my security from any early age, and I've always looked to God in prayer and through reading the Scriptures and trusting Him. Nothing provides me with more security than knowing that God has my back and protects me daily. Quite honestly, God has protected me from women who were not my wife, and potentially life altering sins and mistakes, which I will visit later. As I continued my stay in New York, I voiced a perplexing statement within: "Finding God in this city is like trying to find a needle in a haystack." I took the statement one step further, trying to find a virgin at my age, in this world, is definitely like trying to find a needle in a haystack! After all, who in this day and age truly wants to keep themselves for marriage? It widely appears that the answer would be "No one," but I do.

Now, I can't sit here and pretend I don't have sexual desires, because I do. However, God has kept me from premarital sex. The opportunity to have premarital sex has not presented itself, and here's the reason why:

Jesus declared in Mark 14:38 (NIV), "Watch and pray so that you will not fall into temptation. The spirit is willing but the body is weak." This verse lets me know that if I keep watch of who I get close to AND pray, I don't have to fall into temptation. You may say, "Well Damien, it's not that easy to just stop talking to women, or to not date and hang out with them." Yes it is. You know what pushes those buttons and gets you aroused. You at least have an inkling of who may be physically attracted to you and what will happen if you get too close.

You're better off paying the price of sacrifice now by not having sex, than to pay the price of consequence later through struggling to raise a child as a single parent, STDs, and not to mention the spiritual and emotional effects. Why have premarital sex if you believe it creates soul ties? Why pay countless dollars in medications for a sexually transmitted disease, when you could have said no that night? Why go through the heartache of a broken heart because you chose not to listen to the Scriptures and the Spirit within to flee fornication?

Some of the reasons I just stated are why I chose early on to abstain from having sex. I had made the commitment to myself when I started college in January of 2003. I promised myself I would not entertain a relationship until I completed my bachelor's degree. I did not want women, sex, being a single parent, or STDs to throw me off course. I had the resolve to meet my goal of obtaining an undergraduate degree, and I did not want anything to deter me from accomplishing this achievement.

I was successful in not allowing my attraction to women get to me while I attended Georgia State University in Atlanta, Georgia. I pranced through those first four years of college with no women vying for my attention. Now, I must note that it took me seven years to complete my bachelor's degree, so it was over those last three years that my journey truly began to take shape.

THE BEGINNING

I left Georgia State University in the summer of 2007, and transferred to Atlanta Christian College (ACC) for the fall semester. At ACC, a fun-loving young woman caught my attention. I don't remember how we met but we became friends pretty quickly. We enjoyed laughs and good conversation. One day, after chapel, as we walked to the school cafeteria, she fell back and started walking behind me. I don't remember what I said to her, but I do remember her response: "You lead and I'll follow." I knew at that moment how she felt about me, and I told myself, "I probably shouldn't get too close."

In Genesis 4:1 KJV (King James Version), it begins, "And Adam **knew** Eve his wife..." in the Hebrew, the word "knew" can mean to become acquainted with. Because this young woman and I had spent much time in conversation, I became privy to information that she likely had not shared with other men. We had become well acquainted with one another because we spent a lot of time with each other in conversation and just hanging out. Little did I know, feelings were beginning to stir, and I kept ignoring the warning signs to stay away. What was the consequence? Getting involved with someone emotionally that I did not have a future with. Moreover, wasting time. And there's no need to waste time if you know that the relationship won't go anywhere. As a result, she got hurt, as did I, because we got close but it did not evolve into a serious relationship. (I will delve more into disobedience later on and the effects it has on the life of a believer.) As history would have it, the friendship reached its demise and our relationship was never the same.

Now some people may read that and say, "Well you're a Christian, so why would you cut someone off if you're supposed to show love to everyone?" Proverbs 4:23

declares that we must guard our hearts for out of it flows the issues of life. There I was having intimate conversations with a woman who was not my wife, sharing the personal issues of our lives with one another. All the while we were being knit together in heart without even realizing it. Two hearts can become intertwined through conversation alone.

Have you ever heard of someone having an "emotional affair?" The situation I shared above, and others like it, is an example of an emotional affair/relationship. Because in an emotional affair two individuals can share so much about their lives with one another that they become inappropriately emotionally involved. Each person carefully lays out the issues of their personal life, and in response the other person starts caring deeply for him or her. That deep sense of care, and consequently responsibility, can evolve into love depending on the length of the relationship.

LADIES TWO AND THREE

After I had cut all ties with lady number one, another woman came into the picture. We too became close, and our connection had a heat to it. In retrospect, I can see that it was only emotional in nature, but at the time I did not realize that. As with the majority of infatuation-based relationships, that one fizzled out quickly.

A third woman entered my life, and she was the one I was "supposed" to marry. It was brought to my attention that this woman liked me. I did not like her, but as time progressed I started talking to her and we got to know each other. A prophet came to me and said, "I believe she is your wife." This is why I believed I was supposed to marry her. I took this to heart and continued conversing with her, but in my spirit I knew that it was not the right time to start any type of relationship with her. This happened during the springtime. This same prophet found out that we had been talking. He told me that if I was not willing to commit to her, that I should not continue talking to her. This young lady went to college in another state. She went back to school that fall and we ceased contact for about two years. During those two years I wrestled with thoughts of marrying her, fears of divorce, and if I was actually willing to commit to one woman. At the two year mark, I reached out to her. She said she was done with me and that she'd rather we not talk to each other at all. The two of us never made it past her liking me or even talks of marriage. For a while, lady number two and I continued to have an amicable relationship, but it never materialized.

Relationships like the ones I've just described would continue to repeat in my life, with at least three other women over the next few years. The cycle would start with me meeting someone. Then, we'd get close through conversation. Then the relationship would end. I can tell you exactly why they all ended: I was not supposed to marry any of those women. I knew within myself, by the Spirit of God, that none of them would complement me as a wife. I was always unsure if each of those women were my wife at the time so the relationship would never progress into anything serious. So to be fair to them, and to myself, I had to end those relationships.

It's as simple as that.

If you are following Christ and living by the Scriptures, you cannot attach yourself to just anyone of the opposite sex. You can't just be in relationships with a guy or a girl just because. Define the relationship: is this friendship? Is this courtship? Will it evolve into marriage? Know what you're getting yourself into before saying yes to that person. Be sure God led you both to each other for the purpose of marriage. Having knowledge of what the relationship is will prevent hurt from taking place. It will allow things to be clear and understood.

As a believer, you cannot allow your feelings to get in the way of your own spiritual growth. That late night conversation with "bae" at his or her house, or wherever, could turn into a touch. That touch could turn into sex. Then, before you know it, your relationship with that person becomes centered on gratifying and satisfying the sinful desires of the flesh instead of reigning over them.

PAUSE: TO REIGN

Let me pause right here to define the word "reign" so you have a better understanding of how to take actions against sexual immorality as we move forward. The word reign means to have royal authority (Merriam Webster Dictionary App).

> 14. "...that you keep the commandment without stain or reproach until the appearing of our Lord Jesus Christ, (15.) which He will bring about at the

proper time—He who is the blessed and only Sovereign, the King of kings and Lord of lords..."
—1 Timothy 6:14-15 (New American Standard Bible)

The word "king" in the Greek is translated into the word *basileus* speaking to the foundation of power, meaning sovereign or king or reign which means "to rule" literally and figuratively.

I want to speak to you, king or queen. I want to make it known that we are royalty and we were created to rule over sexual immorality. You have royal authority. Royalty is in your blood. Knowing that you have the ability to rule over something is no small thing! Just realizing THIS as I have been walking on this journey as a single man, has caused me to see how much power I have through Christ! Just knowing that I am a king, has caused me to view myself a lot differently. It has led me to make different choices when it comes to people of the opposite sex. It has caused me to listen to God more and listen less to myself. This revelation alone has changed what I think and subsequently how I act.

RESUME

I thank God that I did not have sex with any of the women that I was in a relationship with. It took me years before I could finally admit to myself that those women and I were indeed in relationships, even if they were never "official" and we didn't use the titles "girlfriend/boyfriend." The enemy is a master at deceiving people into thinking that intimate conversation is harmless, and does not have to lead to anything physical. This is a trick of the enemy. Do not fall for it! I have to remind myself of this constantly. It can be so easy to lose yourself in a conversation, not realizing that it could lead to something more.

I'm truly grateful because had I involved myself sexually with any of those women, I would not be able to write this book that you now read. I would not be able to offer you hope. I firmly believe that my journey, and status as a man who's never had sex with a woman will help show a generation of people that they can maintain purity in a culture that accepts the opposite.

It is my prayer that as this book continues to unfold, that you will gain an understanding of how to maintain your purity (as a virgin or as someone who is celibate) in today's culture. May you be strengthened and encouraged in the pages that follow to live a life of purity unto the Lord as a single person, or until He sends you a wife or husband, and may you continue to do so even after marriage.

CHAPTER TWO

A DEEPER MEANING

We all share the dream of finding "the one," falling in love with that person, getting married, and living happily ever after. We are bombarded with reality shows that fantasize about romantic relationships. Some of us dream about being swept off of our feet in a wave of love, and riding into the sunset with our knight in shining armor, or our princess with the matching glass slipper.

To live in a world of fantasy may be comforting to some, but for others it may represent false hope. It's easy to see such fancies as false hope when all your college friends have gotten married and had children, and seem to be living a great life, all while you walk the earth alone and single. Single and depressed. Depressed because you have not found the one that God has for you.

Every year you hear another preacher say that this is your year. This is your year to walk into the promises of God and to get the blessings that God has for you. Yet what happens when year after year you don't see the blessing of love happen for you? What happens when the woman or man you thought you would marry breaks up with you, moves to another state, and then marries someone else?

You see this part of life is what a preacher may not talk to you about in his or her sermon. The part of life where you reach adulthood and the accountability partners cease contact with you and you are left to fight the enemy by yourself. How hard is it to fight off the demons of premarital sex, anger, depression, bitterness, unforgiveness, and loneliness with no prayer partner there to help you overcome? It's very difficult indeed, but you have to be encouraged that God still has your best interests at heart. You must remember that though you dream of getting married, God may be deferring that dream for a time. There are likely still some things God wants to work out in you before you can meet the person He has for you.

MY PLAN, YOUR PLAN

As a child, I just knew that I wanted to be a doctor. If you were to ask my father today, he would tell you that as a child becoming a doctor is all I talked about. When I first enrolled at Georgia State University, I signed up to be a Pre-Med Biology major. However, once I failed my chemistry course, I knew that medical school was not in my future. As a result of this sudden academic failure I took the time to really seek out what I wanted to major in. I found my passion to be music.

Many people may think changing my major from Pre-Med Biology to Music sounds absurd. I had a mentor hang up on me when I told him of my decision. We never spoke again. I did not have any education in music prior to college. Still, there remained an innate drive to be around music and to learn about it.

Once I decided to pursue music as my major, I never looked back. I tried to get into the Georgia State University School of Music twice over the course of a year, but I was turned down both times. I looked for an on-campus job in production or anything music related but nothing turned up. I took a music business course during a summer semester but I was abruptly dropped from the course. Then one day, my pastor at the time suggested that I look into Atlanta Christian College (ACC), a small, private institution that was only a few minutes away from where I was living. I applied for the music program at ACC, and I was accepted! The rest, as they say, is history.

The bible says in Proverbs 19:21(NIV), "Many are the plans in a man's heart but it is the Lord's purpose that prevails." I had made plans to become a medical doctor, but God had other things in mind for me to do. The same goes for single men and women who desire to be married. I have wanted to get married since I was 19 years old. I've "talked" with many women but none of those "friendships" led to solid relationships or marriage. I recently celebrated my 32nd birthday, and I am still single. Although I still dream of marriage, and desire a godly woman to become my wife, I know I have to wait until God wills my marriage to take place.

OUR VISION VS. GOD'S VISION

Many women may go around saving up thousands of dollars for their dream wedding dress. These same women often plan out who they will invite to be a part of their bridal party. They fantasize about destination weddings, and tell all of their loved ones that they want to be married before they turn 30 years old. And women aren't the only ones. As a matter of fact, I said to myself that if I was not married by the time I turned 30, I would either adopt a baby, or buy a dog. Let the record show, I have not done either of the two.

Most of us are familiar with the vision board trend. People who have vision boards may get a poster and cut out images from magazines or newspapers that represent certain dreams and aspirations. Meaningful quotes/sayings often go on this vision board as well. This vision board is then placed in plain sight to view on a regular basis. This helps keep the creator of the vision board focused on everything he/she wants to accomplish, over the course of one's life or by a certain time. Believers may liken the idea of vision boards and may even reference Habakkuk 2:2-3(KJV) which declares:

> 2 *And the Lord answered me, and said, "Write the vision, and make it plain upon tables, that he may run that readeth it. 3 For the vision is yet for an appointed time, but at the end it shall speak, and not lie; though it tarry, wait for it; because it will surely come, it will not tarry."*

With these verses in mind, many of us, as believers, go about our lives writing down what God tells us. We keep these things before us as a reminder of what God has said to us, and what we hope to see Him fulfill in our lives. What happens though when what God has shown us does not happen when we want it to happen? Do we wallow in sadness? Do we go out and make it happen for ourselves on our own? And in the process obtain some thing(s) we weren't supposed to have? Do we covet what others have or find ourselves discontent when we compare our lives to others? Or should we patiently wait on the Lord and ask Him to show us what we should do while we wait?

Even when we write down "the vision," the Scriptures declare we must wait for the appointed time for the vision to come to pass, or to happen. No matter how long, we must wait for it. The Scriptures remind us that it will SURELY come to pass. The Scripture doesn't say, the vision might come to pass, it says the vision WILL come to pass and it will not tarry or delay.

You see though we may fantasize and go about making lavish and outrageous plans for our lives, ultimately it is God's purpose for our lives that will stand. It does not matter if the preacher hollers at the top of his lungs: "THIS IS YOUR YEAR!" Trust me when I tell you that God is Sovereign and when He is ready to allow something to happen in your life, it will, and nothing can stop it. But it will only happen at HIS appointed time, and not a second sooner, or later.

Our society places so much emphasis on love, and

finding the "One," which for Christians translates to finding a wife or husband. We hear so much about love that a person can lose focus of things like purpose, long-term goals, passions, and dreams. I have watched relationships and marriages lead people down the wrong path in their lives because they get too caught up in the other person or with the wrong person. Love, and everything that comes with a significant other, can often blind a clear mind from other important aspects.

As I mentioned in the previous chapter, I made the commitment to myself not to get into a relationship with anyone until I graduated college with my Bachelor's degree. I did not want a baby, a woman, a sexual transmitted disease, or anything else to keep me from reaching that goal. Within these years of formal education, God began to show me my calling, and how He wanted me to use the gift(s) He'd given me. I learned to seek God for identity and purpose—who I am in Him, not who I am in relation to a woman. Your identity is attached to who God says you are, and relationships can sometimes cloud that judgment if they are not godly. I was able to figure out who I am and what God wants me to do with my life through much prayer, reading the Bible, and taking the time to get to know myself. If I had let feelings for the wrong woman come into the mix, my life would not be where it is today.

Whether you are a virgin, or practicing celibacy, God may have allowed you to remain single so He can show you why He created you. God has a plan for your life and He wants to show you what HIS will is for you. Yes, His will for your life—not your dreams, not what people say you should do, and not even what your parents want you to do. In this time of singleness, allow God to keep your heart, mind, and body pure, so He can reveal your life's purpose. As He reveals His purpose for your life, I pray that you be at peace with His will. Accepting God's will is not always easy at first, but it will bring clarity to your existence and more importantly, help others too.

THE VIRGIN MARY

The Biblical story of Jesus being born of the virgin Mary has been passed down throughout history. Although unfathomable to the finite mind, this story can be grasped and believed through faith. In Luke 1, we read that God sends the angel Gabriel to Nazareth, a town in Galilee, to Mary, a virgin engaged to a man named Joseph. In verse 28, Gabriel announces that Mary is highly favored and that God is with her.

Let me pause right here to share something with you, believer. There have been many times in my own life when I wondered why I remained as I was (not knowing a woman sexually). But thank God I no longer lack understanding. God is with you and me, I firmly believe that. Keeping one's sexuality in tact (not having sex at all), today is rare, especially for a man my age. However, I know that by living this way, God can do great things through a pure vessel. Because I have made the decision to abstain from premarital sex, I am "prepared for every good work" just as 2 Timothy 2:21 declares. When Jesus was on earth,

He was able to do great things because He did what God told Him to do. On this journey to save yourself for marriage, you have to believe that God is with you. Society may frown upon your choice, but God applauds it.

There was something great that Mary had to do, and she would not have been able to do it if she was not a virgin. God needed a virgin for His plan to be executed the way He designed. As the story continues, Luke 1:29 says that Mary was greatly troubled and wondered what kind of greeting this was. Gabriel calmly stated, "Don't be afraid, for you have found favor with God." Mary did not have to fear the angel and the message he carried. For those of us who choose to remain virgins until we are married, we cannot be afraid of the message in the Bible or why God desires us to remain this way. There is favor with God that is attached to this walk of virginity and celibacy. Yes, just because you are a virgin, because you choose to abstain, you have favor with God!

The Greek word for favor is *"charis," which can be translated* graciousness. The word favor is also linked to words such as: acceptable, benefit, grace, gracious, joy, and liberality[1]. The primary benefit that I continue to experience as a man who's never had sex, is knowing that I am pleasing God, and that He is with me. This definitely does not mean that God is not with those who have had premarital sex, not by any means. However I believe that God can work through a vessel of purity to accomplish His will the way

---

[1] Strong's Concordance

He designed it. The word gracious according to the Merriam Webster's Dictionary can mean godly, marked by tact & delicacy, merciful, and compassionate. The gift of virginity is a delicate one, and it should be cherished. It's not enough to give such a precious gift to just anyone. In order to give a good gift, there must be careful thought, consideration, and effort that goes into the giving process. The gift of virginity also has a purpose. Every gift is designed to bring joy to the person receiving it, and every gift is best when it is used for its intended purpose. The joy that comes from waiting to have sex can only come from God. Seek out that joy by remaining pure because the benefits can be life changing for you and the people you are called to influence.

The story of Mary continues with the angel Gabriel explaining to Mary that she will give birth to a son, who she is to name Jesus. "He will be great, and God will give Him a throne and reign over the house of Jacob; his kingdom will never end," Luke 1:31-33 records. Mary's response was, "How will this be?" Gabriel explains that the Holy Spirit would come upon Mary, overshadow her, and that the holy baby she will give birth to will be called the Son of Man. Gabriel concludes by stating that, "Nothing is impossible with God." To which Mary replies: "I am the Lord's servant, let it be according to thy word."

ACCEPTANCE

Mary accepted her calling as the Lord's servant. Mary accepted the message from Gabriel, and what God wanted to do through her. Can you accept the call to remain a virgin, or to remain celibate, so that God can do something great through you? It is not impossible for the Holy Spirit to use you in a way that can change the world!

Think about the example you have set so far and what that could mean for those around you. Your decision to remain pure could change a person's perspective on how they view their body and how others treat them. Your commitment to be bold, and to stand for what God says is right, could birth a movement of purity the world has never seen before. Your example to stay pure before the Lord, can teach others how to reign over sexual immorality just by your choices.

Sit with God in prayer and allow God to show you the purpose behind your virginity or celibacy, and the benefits it will bring not only you, but also the people He wants you to reach. When God shows you the big picture, it will change your life and push you towards purpose in a way you've never dreamed or imagined. Let acceptance be the first step to seeing how God will use you for His glory.

CHAPTER THREE

PURPOSE DRIVEN

Currently, I am at a pivotal moment in my life. I just finished grad school and like many people I find myself thinking, "Now what?" Our society has a set path for young people — get a college degree and find a job. However, the current economy has made job searching quite difficult. But I think the problem is deeper than that. Finding a steady job is one thing, but what if that job is not fulfilling? What if that job is not what you're supposed to be doing with your life? I have realized the dichotomy that my generation faces: tent-making vs. living out the calling God has on your life.

As of late, my mindset has been leaning towards one of purpose. I have been exploring different money-making job opportunities, because I want to use my income, not only to live but more importantly, to fund the calling on my life. The book of Acts records the Apostle Paul's occupation as tent-making (Acts 18:3). But as we know Paul was more than a tent-maker; he was chosen by the Lord to bear His

Name (Acts 9:15). Paul, whose name was once Saul, used to persecute those who followed Jesus (Acts 9:1-5); but then one day, on the road to Damascus, Jesus spoke to him. Jesus told Paul that he would be led to a city where he would be told what to do. After his encounter with Christ, Paul got up from the ground with his eyes open, but he could not see. Those who were with Paul led him to the city. It was there that God spoke to another disciple, a man named Ananias, in a vision concerning Paul. Ananias later found Paul, laid hands on him, then Paul regained his sight and was filled with the Holy Spirit. This marked the starting point of Paul's ministry. Paul began to preach the Gospel.

My journey as a student crossed paths between academia and church life. I went to college to learn everything I possibly could about music, but that also paralleled with my beginnings as a minister at my church. It was through these initial experiences that my heart and mind were opened to the calling God has on my life. Although I did not truly understand it at the time, I realize now that during that period I began to come into my own. Singing on stage both at school and at church were both brand new experiences for me because I had never done anything like it before. It was exciting! It was a new world where people around me were like me; we loved and shared a passion for the Lord and music.

I started writing songs in 2005. I had no clue that 11 years later I would still be writing songs and the type of impact those songs would have on people. The songs I wrote spilled over into my work as the minister of music at my church, where I led worship using the songs God had given me. I realized these songs were to benefit His people.

THE METHOD BEHIND THE MUSIC

As I wrapped up my undergraduate degree, I applied to two graduate schools: Regent University and Liberty University. Both universities accepted me, but I chose to go to Liberty University. My first Masters Degree was in Worship Studies: Leadership. It was during this time that I relearned the biblical principles of worship. This degree helped give me further meaning as to the *why* behind leading worship, writing songs, and ministering. The *why* is simple—it is all to give glory back to God (1 Corinthians 10:31).

The songs I write are not just melodies that I sing in my heart to the Lord (Ephesians 5:19), they have also been written to teach others about Christ and how to live for Him (Colossians 3:16).

This understanding gave my gift of songwriting purpose and real meaning. It is through the songs that God continues to give me that I can write to you about how to live as a follower of Christ. Maybe you are not called to preach the Gospel like Paul, or be a songwriter like me, but everyone has a gift (1 Corinthians 7:7, 1 Peter 4:10). It is up to you to find out what that gift is and how God wants you to use it.

SEEK THE LORD

When God closed the door for me at Georgia State, I had to seek Him through prayer to find out what He wanted me to do. It was not easy, but I let my passion for music guide my decision making. Thank God I did because following His leading has changed my life.

Never in my wildest dreams could I have imagined that I would be recording music and serving in leadership at my church. The way I view life now is completely different from my past perspective. I thank God that He has opened up my understanding about my calling and gifts. This continued understanding only comes through much prayer, study of the Scriptures, and listening to God.

Listen to God. You choose who you listen to, and if you are not listening to God, then you're listening to yourself or others. When you listen to people (yourself included) who are not being led by the Spirit of God, then you could end up living in a way contrary to God's will for your life. God's desire for you is an expected end, filled with hope and a future (Jeremiah 29:11). This expected end requires you to obey what God is telling you to do!

If we don't listen to God we will find ourselves being pulled in different directions. Society will try to pull you one way, your family and friends another. Add your own thoughts to that mix and it can turn into complete chaos because you are not sure which way to go. In those moments, take a deep breath, steal away to your room, close the door, and seek the Father for His direction. God will not only guide your next steps in life, He will also guide the relationships in your life. The people around you could help determine where you end up, and that is a dangerous thing. You cannot give people that kind of power over your life. God has already given you the power to determine where your life goes based on the choices you make, good or bad. Your choices must line up with Scripture and the Spirit of God. Your dreams and desires must be submitted to God, when they are, you will find that your life lines up with the will of God. Your life, and where you end up, is hinged on two things: God's desire for you and your willingness to submit to that desire.

If you pray for direction and He gives it to you, don't turn away from it. Embrace it! If you walk away from what God shows you, it will only eat away at you until you finally do what He tells you to do.

I look at people who don't believe in God and yet I see how hard they go after their dreams and goals. They don't hold back! They believe in themselves and their cause so much that they are willing to run after it, no matter the cost. How much harder should we as believers be going after those things that God has shown us? You cannot allow fear to drive you to a place of zero productivity. When God shows you who you are, believe Him! When you hear that still, small voice saying write that book, record that song, start that business, or you are a preacher, or a doctor, do whatever it takes to become that.

As you seek God be mindful of the different ways He speaks to us. The answer to your questions could come in the form of dreams. Or, people recognizing a certain quality about you constantly could be a hint. What you are called to do could very well be directly linked to what you love to. However, it could also just be something you are naturally gifted at doing well. If people are always coming to you to bake a cake for their next party, or if people regularly call you for advice on life, whatever it is, pay attention. Those are just a few examples of the many endless things that a person can be gifted in and called to. To identify your thing, you just have to do some soul searching.

It took me years to realize that music and everything related to it would be my future tent-making occupation. I feel at home when I am singing behind the piano. There is nothing I want to do more than to serve humanity with my God-given ability to write songs.

I can't explain to you why things happen the way they happen, but I do know that all things work together for good to them that love God, to them who are called according to HIS purpose! (Romans 8:28) His purpose, remember that. My experiences of transferring colleges led me to find out what my purpose in life is. If I did not find my reason for living, there is no telling where I would be. There is nothing more fulfilling in life than doing what you were created to do!

When you seek God and find Him (Jeremiah 29:13), He will start to show you what He has prepared for you (1 Corinthians 2:10-11) but it is up to you to put in the work and follow through. The more time you spend with God in prayer, the more He will show you and tell you what direction you should go in. Yes, seek wisdom from wise people, but at the end of the day, every person has a gift and every person has a calling. Once you find out what yours is, let that be your focus.

THE FOCUS

When God shows you your calling and what He wants you to do with your gifts, it may seem crazy at first but walk it out. Write that vision down, look for people who are wise in your field and get advice from them on what to do. Let the Holy Spirit guide you because your calling originates with Him and it will keep you focused.

Recently, I have been more purpose driven than ever. Nothing matters more to me than fulfilling what God has placed in my heart to do. The moment I decide to do something else other than what is related to God's calling for my life, the inactivity starts to nag at me.

As I walk the corridors of my current job, I have to remind myself that where I am now is preparing me for where God ultimately wants me to be. I work for a package delivery company, and I often say that one day this place will ship my albums. I also said after coming back from a two-week vacation last year that my time here is almost up. I just know that my time there is coming to an end. Where I am now is not my end game. You have to be careful not to get stuck in one place too long, especially if that is not where your calling will flourish. There are certain places that you are only meant to be in for a particular amount of time. Once God is finished teaching you what you need to know within a certain environment, take what you learn and bring it with you to the next place God leads you.

You are probably wondering why I devoted an entire chapter to writing about purpose in a book about maintaining your virginity or celibacy. Colossians 3:1-5 (NAS) declares,

> *"Therefore if you have been raised up with Christ, keep seeking the things above, where Christ is, seated at the right hand of God. Set your mind on things above, not on the things that are on the earth. For you have died and your life is hidden with Christ in God. When Christ, who is our life, is revealed, then you also will be revealed with Him in glory. Therefore consider the members of your earthly body as dead to immorality, impurity, passion, evil desire, and greed, which amounts in idolatry."*

There is a lot to unpack within this passage of Scripture. First, you MUST keep seeking things above. Set your mind on things above where Christ is, and not anything related to this earth. Marriage is an earthly thing. Marriage is for companionship, producing children, and maintaining and building a life with a lifelong partner. After we die, marriage won't exist (Matthew 22:30). We get so caught up in finding love and marrying someone, that we lose focus on what's important to God. God wants us to spread the Gospel throughout the earth and be about His business (1 Corinthians 7:32). Your end game has to be heaven and living in eternity with God. Focus on God's presence in your life, heaven on earth so to speak. When you set your mind on God and things above, what goes on in the world will be of little significance to you. Keeping your mind on things above will keep your mind on the Spirit and not on the flesh. Your desire for sex will constantly fight against your desire to walk like Jesus. If you're focused on things above, where Christ is, the desire for sex can be shifted into a desire to please God with your body.

Second, your life is hidden with Christ in God. There is no life without Christ. Apart from Him, you can do nothing (John 15:5). So everything about you—from who you are to what you do with your life can be found in Jesus' life.

Third, you have to put to death the members (or "desires" as Colossians 3:5 AMP says) of your earthly body. Though the desire for sex is natural, you have to put that desire to death if you don't want to have sex before marriage. This is not an easy task but it can be done. Focusing on things above and things of the Spirit can aid in keeping your mind from wandering to places it shouldn't go. The Spirit of God will remind you, it may come in the form of a quiet inner voice that says, "I shouldn't watch this," or "It's late, maybe I don't need to text her." Walking in the Spirit, or walking the way Christ did, will always lead you back to living according to the Scriptures. You have to remind yourself, or let God remind you, that though your physical body may want sex before marriage, it will not be pleasing to God to partake in such activity.

Allow the calling of God to keep you focused on the will of God for your life. God's desire for you is for you to spend forever with Him, and that you arrive at your expected end here on earth. What you do today will determine where you end up in this life and the one to come. It is imperative that you seek God for your purpose and the way He wants you to live. Your calling is not just related to a paid occupation but to following Christ wholeheartedly. When the desires creep in or opportunities present themselves to sleep with someone, you have to ask yourself would Jesus approve of this? How would this affect the people that look up to me? How would this affect my relationship with God?

The greatest commandment declares that you should love the Lord your God with all your heart, and with all your soul, and with all your mind, and with all your strength. When it comes to your heart and mind, living for God in what you do, will mean the world to you. When by God's grace you start getting yourself together and weeding out the things that God doesn't approve of, even the smallest wrongs will start to convict you. When you begin to match your life up with what you are called to do, premarital sex won't mean that much to you. You will want to put all of your strength, time, and energy into living for God and anything linked to what you're supposed to do as His child.

Seek the Lord, find out what your calling and gifts are, and get to work! Get that tunnel vision going and allow the Light to lead you in the right direction. Keep pressing toward the mark for the prize of the high calling of God in Christ. Let pleasing God with your life become your focus, so that when you get before the Lord He can say, "Well done my faithful servant, with you I am well pleased," (Luke 3:22).

CHAPTER FOUR

MAINTAINING YOUR FOCUS

"And he led Him up and showed Him all the kingdoms of the world in a moment of time. And the devil said to Him, 'I will give You all this domain and its glory; for it has been handed over to me, and I give it to whomever I wish. 'Therefore if You worship before me, it shall be Yours.' And Jesus answered to him, 'Get behind Me, Satan! It is written you shall worship the Lord Your God and serve Him only.'"
— Luke 4:5-8 (NAS)

This Scripture focuses on a pivotal moment in Jesus' journey. Jesus had just been baptized by John the Baptist, and right after, the Spirit of the Lord led Him into the wilderness. While Jesus was in the wilderness fasting for 40 days and 40 nights, Satan comes on the scene and begins to tempt Jesus. Satan tempted Jesus to see if He would bow down and worship him. Just as the Son of Man was not exempt from temptation, neither are we as believers.

DISTRACTIONS

Every person struggles with sin; however, not every struggle is the same. One person's area of weakness may not be someone else's area. Sexual sin is something that many of us deal with on a daily basis. The lure of sexual sin is quite enticing and causes people to become intertwined and entangled with each other. It is enticing because sexual urges are natural and they feel good. Sexual sin is also enticing because of curiosity. I also believe it is enticing because Satan makes it look very attractive. The opposite sex looks good. One wants to engage in conversation with the opposite sex. If a man or woman is physically attractive, you may even go as far as to seek to sleep with that person. The sex that results from this quest can leave one distracted for some time. Sex is something meant to be enjoyed in marriage. This being the case, if one can't have something, it tends to become that much more attractive.

When people (who are single) engage in sexual activity of any kind, I believe they can get lost in each other. Falling in love, infatuation, lust, mutual attraction can all lead to sex. Your life could then become all about being with that person who you're engaging with sexually. Then your focus may begin to slip away from the more important areas in your life.

I have watched sexual sin annihilate marriages, bring down presidencies, destroy careers, tear apart congregations, and make a mess of a person's life. Do not allow it to do the same to you. Our lives and our bodies are important and are of value. No time should be wasted by getting entangled and intertwined with people that keep you in a constant relationship with sexual sin.

I firmly believe that the temptations Jesus endured were necessary. I also believe that temptation takes place to test one's devotion to the Lord. Jesus did not bow down to Satan. Jesus knew the Scriptures and recited them as a defense against the devil's tactics.

The world and its ruler (Satan) are quick to present the fading splendor and glory of sin to get you to believe that doing things your own way should be your end game. Through society, and its different mediums, the enemy presents everything in the world to you and tells you: "You can have it." What isn't always as clear, is the condition with which this offer is made: "Give yourself to me," Satan says. What the devil will never tell you is that once you give yourself to something, anything (sin included), you become a slave to it. (Romans 6:17-19 NAS)

What does it look like to be a slave to a distraction or more horribly, an addiction? Well, every waking moment is driven by what a person must do to meet the need that the distraction or addiction fulfills. If you are distracted by something, that means your focus was on something else before the distraction came.

Two questions now come to mind: 1. What is your focus, and 2. What is your distraction? If you follow Christ, He must be your focus. As a disciple of Jesus, you must follow Him and His commands. Following Jesus means walking in His footsteps (1 Peter 2:21 NAS).

Jesus knew what He was called to do, according to

Luke 5:18-19, and He set out to do it right after he was tempted by Satan. By the time Jesus makes it to the Garden of Gethsemane, on the night of His betrayal, we read that He struggled with the cup (the lot He had been given by God). Still, He surrendered to the will of the Father and Jesus accepted that He had to die.

As followers of Jesus, the struggles of identifying our calling and dying to the desires of our flesh are probably two of the major struggles that we will all encounter. We search for our individual purpose through education, working different jobs, taking on the family business, or taking on whatever feels right in the moment. Still, we must remember the question: "What am I called to do?" can only be answered by God. Once you find this answer, the challenge becomes not allowing distractions to keep you from fulfilling your purpose.

It is so easy to get sucked into the education vacuum because as children that's what we are raised to believe is the right path. As children we are taught that a good education is the way to a great job and success. But what happens when the major you pursue, or even complete, does not match with the gift you have or the purpose for your life? Did the path of education take you away from what you were called to do?

Working a regular job is something that I do not enjoy doing. I am currently in a season where the pursuit for my calling and walking that out is at an all time high. There is nothing that I would rather do more than to record the songs I've written. Currently, the one obstacle in my way is a lack of money. I was not born into a family that had much financial wealth, this has caused me to carve my own path into the music industry as an independent record label owner and artist. I have also found that working at a major company can be a major distraction. Because while I spend all my time on the clock helping someone else achieve their dreams, I find there is little time left to me that I can use to pursue what God has given me.

At any cost we must remember that although working to make a living is a part of life, we must still put in the effort to seek God for His calling on our lives. Once God reveals your purpose to you, do not allow anything to get in the way of you pursuing it. Living out your purpose will yield much reward for yourself and others. With money, education, the opposite sex, and everything else trying to distract you from God's will for your life, you must stay focused. No one can afford to waste any time on something that is not geared towards the fulfillment of their purpose.

DEATH TO FLESH

Dying to your flesh is a topic I really want to address. The struggle and temptation to sin is something this world will never be free of until Christ returns in glory. So what should we do when we are tempted to sleep with someone? Or everything is constantly vying for our attention? What happens when women want to have sex with you but you've made a commitment to the Lord not to have anymore sex until you're married? What do you do when men are constantly trying to get your attention but you know that right now your only focus needs to be on strengthening your relationship with God?

Wanting to fulfill the natural desires of my sex drive has been a struggle for me. I am not married and I have made the personal commitment to not have sex until I am married. Still, the struggle with temptation to engage in sexual activity has become quite challenging.

Sins such as pornography, masturbation, homosexuality, adultery, lust, fornication, and perversion have all attacked this generation. Sinful nature has caused some believers to practice such things in secret, while unbelievers openly make the same things a part of their daily life.

Colossians 3:5 (NIV) reminds us that we must put to death the members of our earthly body: sexual immorality, impurity, lust, evil desire, and covetousness which is idolatry.

Most of my friends, and people I went to college with, are married. I am literally surrounded by close friends that are all married, with the exception of two or three people. One evening after work, I walked into the home of the married couple I was living with at the time. They had invited another couple over and they were all discussing common marital things. After greeting everyone, I went into my room, closed the door, fell to my knees, and cried out to God. I was overwhelmed with my desire for a wife. As I prayed about how I felt, I realized one thing: wanting what someone else has is covetousness...and even more dangerously, it is idolatry.

Most believers who engage in the activities Colossians 3:5 lists will never admit, or even realize, that having sex outside of marriage is idolatry. According to Matthew 5:28, living in a manner that is impure, or even just looking at a woman lustfully is adultery.

So what is idolatry exactly? Idolatry is allowing something else to take the place of God, and worshipping that person, thing, or image. Here's an example that will better illuminate my point. Accessing pornography is very easy in this day and age. In earlier times, a person would need to walk to the convenience store to buy a pornographic magazine. Or a person would stumble across their uncle, cousin, or father's stash of videotapes and PlayBoy. Those were the typical introductions to pornography. The explicit content on these videos and centerfolds would open the mind to a brand new world that seemed to jumpstart puberty in your teenage years. Of course this would also spark sexual interest in you that you likely did not experience prior to that.

Now fast forward a few years. Let's say you're the person in the scenario above, and at this point of the story you are in your early twenties. You're out celebrating your best friend's 21st birthday. He comes up to you and says: "Alright, this is it! We're going to the strip club! We 'bout to turn up, it's gon' be lit!" You're awakened the next morning by the urge down below to have sex. You call up the girl at your job that's been trying to get your attention for the last few weeks, and tell her you just want to hang out. You say you want to hang out, but really you want to have sex, and, in this instance, so does she. She agrees to hanging out, so the two of you go out to dinner, and then go to watch a movie. The date has now come to an end as you approach her place. Now, the two of you are parked in front of her apartment. You begin to kiss, and the opportunity to have sex with her presents itself. What do you do?

What you, or the hypothetical person in this scenario, failed to realize is that trip to the strip club a few nights back caused your mind to be flooded with images of naked women. So when you woke up the next day, that was all you could think about. Let's say prior to your friend's "birthday turn up" you made the decision to keep yourself pure before the Lord, but that strip club experience was your one mess up. The enemy did a phenomenal job of getting you distracted by filling your mind with nothing but images of naked women. You want to do right but all you can think about is doing wrong. All those years of Playboy magazines and adult content has your mind on Cloud 9 sexually speaking. The sexual images you've seen constantly replay in your mind. Images of men and women alike have you burning downstairs with lust and passion. The enemy has done a successful job in keeping those images at the forefront of your mind. Those images have you focused on earthly things instead of the heavenly things above. Of course you did not intend for things to get this far, but they just did. It's a Paul-like struggle where the good you want to do you don't do, but the sin within lures you to fulfill the enemy's desire (Romans 7:19-20 NAS). This is what idolatry can look like if you're not careful. The enemy's desire is that we would worship him, and that we would place our sex drive and all things sexual before God. And if you're not careful that can become your lifestyle. In today's culture sexual immorality, and anything related to it, is totally acceptable. Technology has made it easier than ever to remain distracted and less focused on God.

It amazes me how a group of people, whether family or friends, can be out to dinner without any actual conversation taking place. Everyone has their faces glued to the screens of their expensive smartphones. Devices have caused close relationships to be severed as people become more intimate with what is at their fingertips instead of the people around them. Before a person knows it, the enemy is devouring their thoughts with what comes across the screen. In this instance it's an image of a naked woman…or man. People secretly plot to feed more of the lust that grows within later on that night. What people fail to realize is that pornography pulls you away in the midnight hour and creates a schism between you and the Lord. Thus the distraction of pornography consumes the mind and as a result people turn their focus to that instead of the Lord.

Satan did not succeed in tempting Jesus, by showing Jesus all He could have. Jesus knew that He had to die physically, and be completely dead to sin in life, in order for you and I to live. The Bible declares that we must be sober, or clear-minded, and watchful because our adversary the devil is like a roaring lion walking about seeking whom he may devour. (1 Peter 5:8 KJV).

As believers we must keep a careful eye out for things

we know will harm us spiritually and throw us off course. If you know that certain friends lead you to have inappropriate conversations, then maybe you should cease speaking to them. If you know that internet browsing can lead you to visit pornographic sites, put a blocker on your browser. After all, the Bible says, "If your hand causes you to sin, cut it off for it is better to go through life maimed than to go into hell with two hands into a fire that shall never be quenched (Mark 9:43 KJV)."

You cannot afford to be distracted by anything because your eternity depends on it. You have to keep Jesus (Psalms 121:7-8 NIV) as your central focus because He will keep you on the straight path of righteousness even when your flesh doesn't want to stay on that path.

The enemy will always try to tempt you with sin, but you must tell the enemy, "NO." I know that it is easier said than done, but you can do it. There is more to it than just simply saying no and dying to the flesh though. There are some practical things that I would like you to take a look at to help you stay clear of distractions and move past temptation. These things will help you in maintaining your purity when the enemy tells you not to.

THE WORD

"How can a young man keep his way pure? By living according to Your word."
—Psalm 119:9 (NIV)

When I first read this Scripture, my eyes became a little more opened and my spirit received more strength. The fight and struggle to live pure before the Lord is a challenging one to say the least. With the natural sexual desire pulling at my loins, the struggle to abstain becomes all the more complicated as time goes on. Moreover, with the enemy lurking to see whom he may devour, my fight becomes even more daunting.

The world today is quite bold in saying that sin is the way to go. Homosexuality is widely accepted, even amongst church goers. Pornography is barely talked about, it's just accepted. Adultery is tearing marriages apart. Fornication is covered by the excuse, "God will forgive me, He knows my heart, let me still do it and keep it on the hush..." And lust wanders from heart to heart, knocking, hoping the door will be opened and the flesh will have the opportunity to partake in all things sexual and perverse. The enemy will convince people to believe that this is the right way to live, because these things are popular and everyone is doing it. DO NOT BELIEVE THE LIE!

Living according to the Scriptures is very unpopular, and even frowned upon in some cases. In other cases, living a life that is holy unto the Lord is respected because there are still true examples of holiness out there. Living by the Word requires you to take a stand for what is right in God's eyes. Especially when your thoughts, society, your family, or the devil tell you, "You better live it up tonight! Live in the moment. You only live once!" What happens when you wake up the next day, and you look beside you, and realize the terrible mistake you've just made? As a believer, shame, grief, conviction, and sorrow will all come your way as a result of sexual immorality. Or perhaps your flesh will tell you to do it again, because the sex was just that good.

The Bible says to flee fornication (1 Corinthians 6:18 KJV). The word "flee" in the Greek is best understood as "to run away." Just like Joseph (Genesis 39:12), we must run from fornication because it is not pleasing to God. The Greek word for fornication is *porneia*, and it is linked to idolatry as Colossians 3:5 states.

Because I've never had sex, I cannot tell you all the negative affects pre-marital sex has on you mentally, emotionally, and spiritually. So I turned to two trusted individuals to give a male and female perspective who can better speak to those affects.

THE MALE PERSPECTIVE:

> *"Fornication as a believer was exactly what Paul explained in Romans 7. 'The things I don't want to do, that is what I do.' In short, fornicating is akin to idolatry because, just like any sin, we are worshipping the god of "self" rather than YHWH.*
>
> *[When you engage in sex outside of marriage] You become driven by this insatiable desire to please yourself, being brainwashed to think 'Man I need some p****,' [and] like a vampire, scouring the night in search of the next victim.*
>
> *This worship of self then turns to worship of the counterpart, man or woman, then inevitably ends*

with the worship of the sex organ of the other person(s).

That's why people will say things like 'He has the best d***,' or "She has some good p****.'

Fornication is not just 'related' to idolatry...it is idolatry itself. Porn stars will perform satanic rituals and deny the existence of YHWH, the true God.

Just like the first century church, we are surrounded with this worship of self. It is drenched in occult practices and uses the 'do as thou wilt' mantra of the satanic church as its fuel."

—Daniel Findlay

When Daniel first shared his perspective, I realized he touched on some points that I had not thought about, including the worship of self. Sex always leaves a person wanting more. As Daniel mentioned, it leaves you in search of your next fill. You don't even realize that all you are thinking about is yourself.

If you've already crossed the line, and slept with multiple men or women, then you know what I'm talking about. For many people who have already had sex, sex becomes something that you just do. In some of these cases, sex is no longer pleasurable, or it becomes an addiction. People have sex so many times that it is no longer something special. Thus, the beauty of sex becomes lost in a sea of lust. The beauty fades into an abyss of death because people use sex for their own selfish gain instead of considering God's intention for the act. Sex is meant for marriage, not for idolatrous recreation.

Virginity was intended to be a gift we give to the one we choose to be our spouse. Laying down your sexual desire to please the Lord is what you should be striving for. Don't allow the popularity of fornication to become your way of living. Don't risk losing something so precious for a moment of pleasure. It is not worth it. You are more valuable than a quick orgasm with a person who is not your spouse. What God has given you in the gift of virginity is meant for one person: your spouse. One person to have and to hold, and a love to display as Christ and the church.

Though the sexual desire is natural, it is important that we practice self-control. This fruit of the Spirit will aid in keeping you from sexual sin. Let the Word of God help you in keeping your way pure so that you may be found blameless in the Lord's sight. It is still possible for you to remain a virgin until marriage, or to be celibate. Don't let anyone tell you that it is not. God will keep you, just continue to read the Scriptures and live by them. The reward will be well worth the wait.

THE FEMALE PERSPECTIVE

"Fornication is an illusion; it's a transaction, with no security, [and] no insurance.

For years, I engaged in these transactions, depositing my time, while making sure to withdraw my heart. That was the only way that I could be sure to protect my assets.

I exalted these moments, first and foremost in my head- 'He's so fine; I've already lusted in my mind, so I might as well do it...' But undoubtedly the floodgates would open with questions instead of blessings- 'How did I allow myself to get here? When did remaining pure stop being enough? Because no one else is doing it? Since when have you followed the crowd??' Fornication led me down a narrow road that was only wide enough to encompass me and The Holy Spirit. He waited for me there until I was tired of hearing myself pray the same repentance prayer. He unveiled to me that there is so much more in store in the 'act of sex' than what I had been receiving. I now look forward to the day when I can consummate with my equally invested partner, my husband, the day when my sexual investments will yield a return—unity, trust, children, compassion and understanding. Those transactions will come out of a for-better-or-worse commitment. There will be no concern of illegitimate children or the need to duck and hide, for the ONE Who created the act will be right by our side."

—Kamilah Smith

Kamilah posed an important question that most people may glance over: When did remaining pure stop being enough? Even within my own personal experience, I did not realize how valuable purity is. It is so easy to foolishly compare my walk with those who have already crossed the line. To even begin to envy a sinful way of living is sin itself. The thought that a person is better in some way because he or she has more sexual experience is absurd. Just because you know someone who has already crossed that line, doesn't mean you know all the consequences and effects that come with that decision.

Kamilah expressed that what she received as a result of having sex before marriage is a myriad of questions instead of the assurance of God's answers. Kamilah experienced a lack of peace and as a result totally withdrew her heart from the act of sex. Kamilah desired trust, unity, and compassion but she did not receive these things in their fullness because she was not married. All of the questions that filled her mind, and her withdrawn heart, kept her distracted from the Source of real love: God. Like Kamilah, many people engage in heartless sexual activity that yields no return. And instead of hearts devoted to God and kept in safety for their future spouses, their hearts are locked away and left to receive nothing at all. No life, no pure love from their betrothed, and no peace.

There is such peace in devoting one's heart and time completely to the Lord. Living in right standing with Him is important. Following the Scriptures, and doing what it says, is spiritually beneficial for us and keeps our focus on God.

What I've come to realize is that because I've decided to abstain from fornication, God is pleased. It is the will of God that we should be set apart for pure living, and abstain from fornication while we are unmarried. This is necessary so we know how to control our body in purity and honor (1 Thessalonians 4:3-4).

PRAYER

The perspectives Daniel and Kamilah shared, bring me to my final point: prayer.

Idolatry, the constant desire for more, the flood of questions, and the countless other ramifications are some of the culminating distractions that come from fornication. Here are several Scriptures that relate to prayer and can help in combating this act of sin.

"Watch and pray, that you enter not into temptation: the spirit indeed is willing, but the flesh is weak."
—Matthew 26:41 (KJV)

Staying watchful is instrumental in staying away from pre-marital sex. Staying watchful includes: not entertaining or engaging in sexual conversation; not being alone with a person in an environment that could lead to sex; having strong believers around you to hold you accountable; and taking in the Scriptures regularly, to name a few. All of these can aid in being watchful, but Jesus didn't just stop with the word watch, He also added prayer.

"Pray without ceasing."
—1 Thessalonians 5:17 (KJV)

Here we find a challenge issued to us by the Apostle Paul. I say "challenge" because a lot of people in the United States would say they live very busy lives, but even so, that does not negate the fact that we must still pray continuously. I try to pray all of the time, especially when I know the enemy is lurking around in various forms. I'll walk around my job praying in the spirit to help strengthen my inner man (1 Corinthians 14:4 NIV). Praying in that way keeps me focused on God, spiritual things, and doing the right thing.

I find it quite powerful that Jesus said that if the disciples watched and prayed they would not enter into temptation. Stop and think about that for a few seconds. While on earth, Jesus was always stealing away to a solitary place to pray. In addition to living by the Scriptures, Jesus showed us that prayer was an integral part of dying to the flesh. The prayers of a righteous man gives you tremendous power from within to overcome the fleshly desire of doing wrong. I know that I could not have made it as long as I have without the power of prayer and the Scriptures to guide me every step of the way.

> *"Walk in the Spirit and you will not fulfill the lust of the flesh."*
> —Galatians 5:16 (KJV)

Having this verse as a constant reminder helps me with little things like: "Ah man, let me not look at her behind." It helps me to keep my eyes on the spiritual benefit the Scripture provides and not on the good-looking woman, because if I look at her long enough, I'll "wanna holla." Then if I go holler at her and she's down for conversation, that could open the door for me to spend time with her, and that could lead to whatever, because both sides have left the door open to temptation.

The more I pray, the more it reminds me to stay away

from the situation I just described above. It pushes me to look within at my problem spots, like lust and other distractions that could lead to sex, that I have to deal with. Prayer helps point the focus back to the cross and dying to the flesh.

SUMMING IT ALL UP
John 12:24 (NAS) declares:

> *"Truly, truly, I say to you, unless a grain of wheat falls into the earth and dies, it remains alone; but if it dies, it bears much fruit."*

If you don't die to the flesh by way of obeying the Word, and staying away from those distractions God convicts you about in prayer, how will you bear fruit?

My ability to avoid fornication has only been accomplished with help from the Holy Spirit. Without the Word guiding my every move, I would have had sex a long time ago. Prayer keeps me even more focused on God.

I must admit that being watchful is something that I must pay more attention to. My desire for sex has increased in this season even as I write these words to you. I know that it is not in the will of God to fornicate and I am grateful that no women are throwing themselves at me. I firmly believe that watching and praying has played a major part in me staying away from women.

You must have the resolve to say no to anything that would keep you from maintaining sexual purity. Don't throw away your virginity for a summer fling or midnight rendezvous. Don't fall back on your commitment to the Lord and to yourself to not have sex just because your family/friends do it or society deems sex before marriage acceptable; keep up with your commitment to the Lord to not have sex before marriage. Don't fall back, because the reward of following through on your commitment to God is greater than the shame, guilt and other feelings that will come because you didn't stick it out. Remind yourself how valuable your body is. Remind yourself that sexual immorality is not pleasing to God, because the Word says so. Say no to your flesh, DO THE WORD, and pray to the Lord all the time. These simple but proven actions will help you to remain focused on maintaining your purity

CHAPTER FIVE

THE DARK SIDE

The reason why certain things happen can be quite a mystery. As I've mentioned earlier, I've wanted to be married since I was nineteen years old. Since that time, over the years, I've had interest in a lot of women and there have been women who have had an interest in me. Yet the recurring question in my mind has been: Why am I not married yet?

In 2016, while visiting New York, I got the idea to write the book you now hold in your hand. It is my firm belief that if I was already married, I would not have been inspired to write this book. Although we may not understand the reason why God does things the way He does them, there is a method to His Will. There is a purpose behind why things happen in our lives the way they do.

Many of us feel that once our testimony is put on display, we will be held to a higher standard. We also believe that everything we do will be put under a microscope. I know I will be held to the standard that I am pushing you to live out. I know that this is the challenge for every believer: to live by the Scriptures and to remain on the narrow path of righteousness. It can be done! After all, Jesus did it. He was tempted with everything we as human beings are tempted with, but yet He was without sin.

I am literally pausing before I write what you're about to read because I have had to uncover some things. The experiences that I will unpack and discuss are extremely graphic and explicit. I caution you that if you are under the age of thirteen to get your parent(s) and read this chapter with him/her/them. Feel free to ask them questions to gain a better understanding of how this may relate to your own life. I do not know the impact these things will have on you or the people in my life; but I have to uncover what has taken place in my life. It is my hope that what follows in this chapter can jumpstart conversations that will help bring healing. Moreover, that these words will help shed some light on a topic not discussed often enough.

CONCEPTION: WHERE IT ALL BEGAN

I was raised by my father from the ages of five through fourteen. My father worked two jobs, one as a chef in a downtown hotel and the other as a bus driver. One night he dropped me off at a lady's house from church. This was some time before I was nine years old. This lady had two daughters, and as was common practice at the time for sharing the bed as children, we slept at opposite ends of the bed.

I remember the eldest of the two daughters reaching for my foot and placing it inside of her panties to rub her vagina. You may be wondering why I am describing my first sexual encounter with you. This encounter marked the conception of all things sexual for me. However, this encounter was actually something much deeper, it was sexual abuse. Some people may say, "Oh, its not that serious." But it is that serious to me. In those days, I was just an innocent child. Neither of my parents had taught me anything about sexuality. I had never seen a woman naked before. I had never touched a girl in a sexual manner. Until that night, in that dark bedroom with no one to rescue me from the hands of my first abuser.

The next two stories mark a struggle that this generation is beginning to embrace. They will shed light on the sexual struggles and temptations I face now, as an adult.

AND SO IT GROWS

Some time after that first sexual encounter, I was dropped off at a family member's house. This family member had a son who was not much older than me. I remember being in a dark, unfinished basement with the pink insolation still showing. The boy took me between the open wooden frames and I remember him sticking his penis inside of my anus. I can recall the smell. I can recall exactly how it felt as he did what he did that day.

I don't remember how I felt afterwards, I just remember that it happened. I remember that I was taken advantage of. A few years ago, I called this abuser in an effort to gain closure for myself. He denied that anything like that had happened, and even went as far as saying someone else must have done that to me, but that it was not him.

What happened to me at that young age affected me deeply. It should have never happened, but it did. The act brought about unwanted and unnatural desires. It caused me to be aroused in a manner that is contrary to the will of God. It still hurts me to know that this happened; and sometimes I still ask God, "Why?" I wonder if this person took advantage of other boys the way he took advantage of me. I wonder if he took advantage of women, and had his way with them, the way he did with me that day. Still, I choose to believe that one day he will have to answer for his actions, even if he denies them to me. He'll have to live with what he's done, and maybe one day he'll own up to what he did.

THE BIRTH OF SOMETHING UGLY

My third sexual abuser happened to be someone close to me. I could never have imagined something so life changing could happen to me by another family member, yet it did. My childhood was still great at this point. I would go outside to play with friends. I went to church. I lived like every child should: care-free. I watched cartoons and G-rated movies. Little did I know, something was about to take place in my life that would change its course, from who I once was to who I would become.

As I would sit on the couch to watch these fun-filled kid shows and movies, my innocence would officially be stripped from me for good. This third occurrence of sexual abuse was the most impactful. It happened more than once, and by the same person. It is this third instance that sparked my major struggles with sexual immorality today.

I remember me sitting on the couch, and this person would sit beside me and reach over to feel my bottom. What's amazing to me is that the enemy will always reach out to you. He will be subtle at first, just to get your attention. At first it feels weird, but because the touch brings your flesh pleasure, your body begins to react to what it feels.

I would say, "Stop. Stop doing that to me," as the touches came. This happened a number of times. However, as time progressed, I would find myself being coerced into sexual activity with him. He would always go first, initiating anal sex with me. I would turn him around and try to do things the opposite way, not knowing what I was doing. I did not know what was happening or the affects it would have on me long term. I remember one of the last times anything sexual happened between us. He ejaculated on me, and I was so disgusted. I told him to get it off of me, and he just sat there and laughed. I was upset that he had his way with me and left his sperm on my body. I was left helpless with no way to rid myself of the dirt that made me feel unclean.

The enemy will draw you in, then leave you helpless with no one there to pick you up. I did not have anyone to run to. There were no church leaders to tell what had been happening to me. I could not turn to my parents to give me comfort. My relationship with God was virtually non-existent at this point so I did not have the knowledge to cry out to Him to save me. I did not know I wanted to be free from this but I knew I was bound. I knew I was trapped into doing this, bending to the will of the spirit that took control of yet another male in my life.

In recent times I called him to ask what made him do those things to me all those years ago. He said quite frankly that he was horny, as most preteens are at that age. Then I asked him another question: "What you did to me, had that been done to you?" With hurt, hesitation, and the response of a little boy over the phone, he replied, "Yes."

It is unfortunate to know that some men, such as my third abuser have been sexually abused by another male or female and will not talk about it. Some of those men may even struggle with homosexuality at some point in their lives, whether openly or in private. These men usually won't tell anyone what past experiences got them to that point. It is evident that most sexual abusers have been abused themselves and continue the cycle because they do not know how to break it.

Sex trafficking, the porn industry, those who participate in stripping, pimping, prostitution, homosexuality, and promiscuity are all sexual immoral in nature. The people who find themselves involved in such things did not get there solely by their own will. They were probably forced, coerced, or enticed to participate in such sexual activity. To be forced to do something and not have a choice in the matter is slavery in itself. The abusers are often dealing with insecurity and have been victimized themselves. They have not found freedom and so they live imprisoned while arresting others and making those people bend to their will.

Some people say that homosexuality is not a choice, but

some people may be living this way because they were abused, molested, or raped by the same sex at a younger age. And so when they reach adulthood they just act on what they feel is natural because that is all they have known. It is possible that some people simply grow into the seed that had been planted in them during childhood. Promiscuity too can be lived out by personal choice; however, people who regularly have sex before marriage could have also been exposed to sexual things early on.

As you read this, you may be wondering why I uncovered such graphic stories of sexual abuse. In order for you to understand my struggles and temptation with sexual sin, you have to understand where it came from. My temptation with sexual sin came from these instances of sexual abuse. Shortly after these occurrences, I visited my mother in Atlanta, and that's when the struggle truly began.

MY NEW LIFE

I ended up moving to Atlanta when I was 14 years old. I was in the thick of puberty, and my sexual desire had increased significantly. Every time I was aroused, I'd try to find some relief and release somewhere. The sexual abuse I had experienced during my childhood had given way to an open road of masturbation.

I remember hearing the same family member who was the last to abuse me sexually, masturbate in the bathroom while one of his male friends was in there with him. He would lock the door so that I wouldn't come in or know what they had been doing. Still, I knew what had taken place.

Once high school began, I was introduced to pornography through some friends. I would bring sex tapes home, or movies with sexually explicit scenes in them and watch them. At this point, masturbation was a normal occurrence. For a while, my brain managed to lock away all memories of my sexual abuse. But then I started having dreams. In these dreams, by third abuser would perform sexual acts on me. Wet dreams would be the end result of these re-lived experiences. Every time I had a wet dream I hated it because I'd have to clean myself up. I did not like sperm on my body. It puzzled me that my third abuser would be in my dreams doing these things to me. I was reliving every sexual occurrence I had with him, but he was not even physically present. The spirit of perversion had stirred up something ugly within me. Not only was I in bondage outwardly—watching porn and masturbating—I was also being raped mentally, through my constant dreams where my abuser often appeared.

I remember wanting the dreams to stop. I was tired of being tormented nightly by my abuser. That was true torment. Not only was I fighting a demonic spirit, but I did not know how to get the demon off of me. The demons wouldn't leave me alone. I did not know how to get the spirits totally away from me. They tormented me day and night. It was a continuous cycle of masturbation by day, then wet dreams at night. I would cry out to God, asking Him to make them stop. He heard my cry, and rescued me. But soon after, another spirit lurked its way into my heart. And all the while, the struggle not to masturbate continued.

MY FIRST TASTE

Atlanta's southern culture is quite different than what I had been accustomed to growing up in Canada. I had never been exposed to that many young black people, in one place at the same time, before attending high school in Atlanta. The black women that surrounded me were very attractive. I loved it! I had a crush on this Hispanic girl all throughout high school. I liked other girls too, but this girl in particular had my heart.

When I was in elementary school, I remember playing with a friend during recess. I don't remember how it all went down, but we kissed. I can't remember if she leaned over and kissed me, or if I was the one who kissed her. It didn't really matter. All I know is that I got a taste of some sugar and I was hooked.

Fast forward to junior high school, I had three girl-friends. The first relationship didn't last too long. However, my second girlfriend, she was everything to me. I can still remember what she looked like, and how cool she was. I probably loved her, although I had no clue what love was because I was still very young. We went out together for a solid year, then we broke up. The next year we went out again, only to break up again. That was my first long-term relationship with a girl, and I enjoyed every minute of it.

My third girlfriend was cute. She had fair skin and her blue eyes were captivating. She had the cutest pixie cut. I loved everything about her. She was meek, quiet, sweet, and easy to get along with. One day we were outside after school, and I shared what I'll call my (second) first kiss with her. That was a moment I'll never forget.

A DIFFERENT STRUGGLE

As my high school years drew to a close, they ended with not having a girlfriend. While most teens at this time have explored their sexuality with full force, or lost their virginity, I didn't engage in any such activity. I attended a state university for four years, knocking out my core classes. I changed majors a number of times before transferring to my alma mater.

Prior to that point, I had no women pique my interest, and none seemed to be interested in me. However, as soon as I set foot on the campus of Atlanta Christian College, women started paying attention to me. It was weird but pleasant. Who wouldn't want the attention of women and new found friends? I was finally a part of a culture I could relate to. I majored in music ministry, and met new friends who also did music.

I did not live on campus, but I did hear of students having sex. I even had close friends who succumbed to temptation, and ended up getting their girlfriends pregnant. Though I had a few relationships with women while in college, things never got serious. I was never physical with them either, so that spared me a lot of the consequences that often come with pre-marital sex.

However, amidst those victories I struggled with homosexuality. I know now that it was linked to the sexual abuse I experienced in my early childhood. On top of that,

I was living in Atlanta, one of the top cities for the LGBTQ community in the country. I remember one night I got off of work and hopped on the train. I saw this guy and struck up a conversation with him. I would often have conversations with random strangers I met on the train about life. I remember giving this particular guy my number, thinking nothing of it, except that it might be a simple witnessing tool. However, he called me that same night, after we had gone our separate ways. The conversation quickly took a turn that I was not expecting when he started asking me if I was sexually active. I told him, "No." Then he said, "So you don't have sex with men then?" I emphatically answered, "Uh, no." He muttered "Alright, then bye," and quickly hung up the phone.

That was the first time I had a guy make sexual advances towards me. I remember when I first started working at my current job, people would call me gay, or think that I was. I truly believe that the enemy left a mark on me. In times past, if I felt like a guy was attracted to me, my body language would change. The spirit within wanted to participate in a deadly game of cat and mouse. If I sensed a man was attracted to me or I knew that a man was gay, my flesh wanted to act on impulse. My flesh wanted to ask for the number. My flesh wanted to be enthralled in passionate lust for a man because then my flesh would be free. I would hear the tempting thoughts tell me that I wouldn't have to worry about pregnancy. The thoughts of how it felt for a man to touch me, or for me to touch him caused my loins to burn. The experiences from my childhood wanted me to once again act them out, but this time in my adult life. It was something that had been trying to get out.

It is not normal in God's eyes to have sexual relations with the same sex according to Romans 1. The church has embraced gay pastors and congregations. The United States government continues to push for equality for the LGBTQ community. It is now considered normal to see a same sex couple holding hands, or existing as a part of our daily lives.

If a generation has embraced being gay, then that means they've failed to fight it. Some people who are homosexual may say that they were born gay, and that it is simply who they are. However, homosexuality is an identity they have embraced, but is it the image God created them in? Or are they living a lie? I will delve more into this topic in the next chapter.

THE STRUGGLE BECOMES ALL TOO REAL

Understand that while I may find a guy attractive on occasion, I constantly remind myself of what is right. Homosexuality is not right in the sight of God (according to Scripture). The culture today is adamant about the rights of people of the same sex marrying each other. Gay churches say they accept those who identify as LGBTQ for who they believe they are.

Do you know how easy it would be for me to carry out a secret life of sex? You don't of course, but let me tell you, it would be very easy. However, I know that if I didn't seek to live according to the Scriptures I could easily have a life enthralled with sex, with both men and women. The enemy is ruthless in his pursuit of men and women who seek to live for God. He will do everything in his power to get you to fall and succumb to temptation. The sexual abuse that I suffered as a child has been very painful to deal with. I've often had to ask the question, "Why did I go through this?" No matter what has happened to me in the past, I've come to the realization that I cannot sin and just be okay with it. Satan will make you think you can sin and that your sin will not find you out. But you have to be willing to stand up when tempted and take the escape route God provides. Take it as soon as it presents itself to you.

Some time ago, I was talking to a young lady. We had been talking for a couple months, when she invited me over to her house, around the holidays. I accepted and went to her house to hang out. At some point, her parents left. Shortly after, I decided to leave. But when I gave her a hug, she would not let me go. The hug lingered. Her hand touched the back of my neck and she gently caressed my hair. I told her I had to go, but she only held me tighter. I realized that she didn't want me to go. For a moment, I gave in and held her close. I smelled her hair. My lips were close to her neck. My hand went to her waistline, and I proceeded to lift up her shirt. I realized what was happening and snapped out of it. I told her, "I have to go." She said, "I don't want you to go." Some time passed but eventually we let go of each other, and I proceeded to my next destination.

As I recall the situation, I realize that in that moment

where I could have allowed things to get physical, maybe we would have even ended up having sex. The fact that she didn't want me to leave, and her parents weren't home, was a perfect opportunity for us to engage each other physically/sexually.

I can remember another time when I was sitting on the couch with a friend from college. She sat inches away from me and I remember the look in her eyes. That look made me think that she was into me. I was close enough to kiss her, and I wanted to, but I'm glad I didn't. And here's why: there is no telling where that kiss would have led. The enemy will lead you to think that a kiss or a hug is no big deal. He would like you to think it's all innocent, but even innocent interactions with physical touch can lead to a baby nine months later. Physical touch of any kind can lead you to the point of no return.

LATELY...

Lately, the sexual tension down below has been at an all time high for me. To have the fire lit, and my man parts rock hard, in the middle of the night with no way to release myself has been challenging to say the least. I can feel my flesh and my spirit warring against each other. The fight against masturbation and pornography has been a constant struggle because of what I was exposed to early in my life. There are days where I overcome and there are days where I have failed miserably. We all struggle with sin, and we all must fight to overcome.

The struggle for Jesus was all too real in the Garden of

Gethsemane. Luke 22 records that Jesus wanted God to take the cup from Him. Drops of blood hit the ground as our Lord and Savior prayed in agony to the Father. Jesus wanted God's will to be done, all while He struggled with His own. And here the real question arises: can you sacrifice your flesh for the generation that you are called to help spread The Good News to? Jesus was struggling, and He made sacrifices as He struggled. Jesus was also strengthened in His darkest hour by angels. At your darkest hour, when you are in your weakest moment, be reminded that God's strength is made perfect in your weakness (2 Corinthians 12:9). Though the enemy may throw things at you, be reminded that you have the power to take the way of escape God has made for you (1 Corinthians 10:13).

That's how I liken my own struggle with sexual immorality as of late, to that of Jesus' struggle in the Garden. On one end I struggle and want to do wrong, but some sacrifices, like the drops of blood that dropped from Jesus' forehead, let me know that I can overcome. To be honest, my struggle with lust has increased. Seeing all of these married couples around me has only been adding to the jealousy and envy in my heart.

As my loins burn in the wee hours of the morning, I have to remind myself that masturbation is something God isn't pleased with. In the end, I'm only pouring out life for it to die in a toilet bowl. God was not pleased with Onan in Genesis 35, when he spilled his semen instead of making a child with it. That example is not a license to go find a girl and have sex with her just so you don't spill your semen like Onan. But you and I both know that semen exists to make a baby, period.

At times it is extremely difficult not to entertain thoughts of fornication related to lust. The seeds that were planted in me by my male abusers have sought to become full grown in my adult life. Though my flesh may want me to act on those unnatural thoughts, I am reminded to think of Scriptures, to think on things that are pure. There is nothing pure, natural, or pleasing to the Lord about fornication, masturbation, pornography, or a homosexual lifestyle. So I fight daily in order for my spirit to win over my flesh.

The temptation to sleep with women has been coming from weird places too. Random women have sent direct messages to me via social media. They send me pictures, ask me for my email address, and more. And as I've mentioned before, with smartphones and the accessibility of the internet, Satan has found a way to get into our minds and mess with us. He will continue to use those devices to keep us captivated with all things sexual, just to keep us distracted from Jesus.

Although my desire for sex has been at an all time high, I don't have women dropping their panties at my feet. Still, the option is there for me to initiate sex if I really wanted to. The fact that the desire is there is all the enemy needs. James 1:14 states that every man is tempted, when he is drawn away by his own lust, and enticed. Then when lust has conceived, it brings forth sin: and sin, when it is fully grown, brings forth death.

The Spirit of God led Jesus into the wilderness without

food. This is where the devil tempted him. The word wilderness in Greek is translated "multitude of spirits." So here I am at 32 years of age, being tempted by homosexuality, lust, fornication, masturbation, pornography, and perversion. All of these spirits have been trying to get my attention, all at the same time. On the other side of this, doors have been opening for me in my ministry. I released a single and started a record label. I've been traveling alongside a man of God, (the prophet I spoke of earlier who told me my journey would be long), leading worship in different cities. I've led worship in different places in the Metro-Atlanta area, Puerto Rico, Jamaica and in Canada too.

So all of these spirits have been looking to distract me, and get me to fall. All of this while serving in ministry. I realize that I'm being tempted just as Jesus was. The devil tempted Jesus, but Jesus did not fall. The Bible says Jesus was tried on every side but still did not give in (Hebrews 4:14-15). Though I have sinned in the areas of lust, masturbation and pornography, by God's grace I have not been sexually active. I have sought the Lord with much diligence to keep myself pure of sexual sin. This has been no easy feat. I am eternally grateful that I have not given in to the enemy's prompts, and that by God's power I have been able to stay away from having sex with women AND men. Even though I was sexually abused as a child, and the enemy has even tried to use that molestation to his advantage, GOD blocked it.

It is only the grace of God, and strength from the Holy Spirit that has kept me from participating in the things I've been tempted with. I have had to pray. I have had to open the Scriptures and remind myself of what not to do. I have had to seek out friends, and counsel, to help keep me on track with the Lord. I have had to shun inappropriate conversations with certain people. I have had to avoid watching certain shows or movies. Because all of these things can feed your sexual appetite if you're not careful. The Bible is clear (Matthew 5:29-30) that whatever causes us to sin, must be cut off! Listen to the Lord when He warns you.

One night while I was working a double shift, an employee said to me, "I'm looking for someone to share Valentine's Day weekend with in a cabin. We don't have to be in love but we can play like we're in love." What this woman didn't know is that my birthday is the day before Valentine's Day. Lord knows my flesh wanted to take her up on the offer.

But then I had a dream. In the dream, I was performing oral sex on this same girl who wanted to spend the weekend with me. She moaned, and even said the name Jesus. When I was finished, I went to the bathroom sink, and proceeded to cough up blood. When I woke up, I asked the Lord what the dream meant. This is the interpretation I received. The blood was a sign of two things: disease and me breaking covenant.

I took the dream as a warning: Don't do anything sexual with this girl or else you will become ill. Also, I didn't want to cheat on my future wife, or be unfaithful to the Lord. The third thing I took away from the dream was the literal coughing up of blood. In order to cough up blood, it would have to come up through the throat. So what if the sickness that resulted from oral sex took place in my throat? Would I be able to preach the Gospel? Would I be able to sing songs unto the Lord? Would I be able to lead people into God's presence through the songs He's given me? In essence, the sickness would have been detrimental to my ministry. Some people may think I'm trying to be deep, but that's what I took away from the dream. There's no telling what the coughing up of blood had in relation to the oral sex. My initial thoughts were that it could've been a STD, that she had, that I ended up contracting. Do you really think losing my voice is worth one night of oral sex with some random woman? NO! The struggle is real, but the consequences from having pre-marital sex are even more real. The dream was enough for me to turn down the invitation and stay clear of the employee.

As you remain committed to the Lord, you have to re-mind yourself that abstaining from sex is about pleasing the Father and keeping yourself pure. Moreover, it is a part of living holy and refusing to be immersed in the cul-ture. Your desire for sex is natural; you will have those urges, but self control must become a normal practice for you in order to reign over those urges. If the temptation becomes all too real and the enemy is at your heels, pray-ing and fasting should be next in order for you to fight off those sexual devils. If you have to cut off social media ac-cess, or limit your time on the internet, or put certain set-tings on your web browser, then do so! Do whatever it takes for you to avoid sexual immorality; cut it off. Face it.

Confront it. Deal with it. Overcome it. Then don't look back. We are more than conquerors through Him that loves us (Romans 8:37). We have victory over sin, we just have to walk in it.

THE END OF IT ALL

At the end of it all—the temptation, the sexual abuse, and everything in between—I still have to serve God. People still need to see an example of purity today. As challenging as it is to remain pure, I still seek to do so daily. I thank God that I don't have women chasing me down, but even that appears to be changing. Even so, I must remain pure and focused on the Lord. Certain songs help me maintain my focus. However, Scripture is the biggest help in abstaining from all things sexual. The Word of God is what will help me keep my way pure (Psalm 119:9).

My brothers and sisters, do not expect temptation to go away anytime soon. It will be present with you until you breathe your last breath, but it is up to you to take the escape route provided by God. Though Satan lurks, seeking whom he may devour (1 Peter 5:8), you can overcome him by living according to the Word. Temptation is there for you to stand up to it, and in doing so, you prove your love for God. When we do what God commands, we show that we love Him (1 John 4:19).

Prove your love to God by fleeing fornication/sexual immorality (1 Corinthians 6:18). You may think you want to sleep with that man or have sex with that woman, but think about how you will feel afterwards. Think about how your decision would displease God, when you knowingly take a route contrary to the Word. Think about the consequences before you indulge yourself in that moment of temporary pleasure.

I am a witness that you can stand in the face of temptation and walk away from it. After all, greater is He that is in you than he that is in the world (1 John 4:4). The God inside of you is greater than that woman dropping her panties in front of you and telling you to come get it. The God inside of you is greater than the pornographic websites trying to get your attention. The God inside of you is greater than the spirit of perversion pushing you towards sexual immorality that is detestable in God's sight. You can overcome, if you're willing to listen to the Holy Spirit, and willing to deny yourself. Denying your flesh will bring you more life than burying yourself in sexual pleasure ever will. Fight. Overcome. Love. Live. Reign.

CHAPTER SIX

DON'T BELIEVE THE LIE

As I was writing this book, and going about my week, I wondered why the temptations I have exist. Homosexuality was lurking its ugly head around the corner, trying to taunt me. Women and their bodies were trying to get my attention. Masturbation called my name in the wee hours of the morning. Still, I refuse to have pre-marital sex by choice. Sex won't be an option until I'm married. However, sexual desire is still present. As I pondered the temptations I face and why they existed, one Scripture reference came to mind:

> *"But every man is tempted, when he is drawn away of his own lust, and enticed. Then when lust hath conceived, it bringeth forth sin: and sin, when it is finished, bringeth forth death."*
> —James 1:14-15 KJV

Now you may think, "Well Damien, how exactly are you tempted?" I briefly alluded to the answer in the last chapter. With men, it's mostly a sexual temptation, but it's deeper than that. Temptation in this area looks like briefly imagining a life as a gay man. Not worrying about having children. Being engulfed in lust and sexual escapades. My flesh roaming free to do as it pleases. With women, the temptation goes further still. The desire for sex is present, but being married to a woman for life is the ultimate goal. Thoughts of marriage seep into my daydreams, along with desires for a family and building a life with someone.

Sometimes counter-productive thoughts creep into my mind. I think maybe I can go to strip clubs and fill my eyes with naked women. But I know this would only feed my sexual desire more, and my body would want sex even more. I would desire sex sooner than my body is supposed to have it. Other times, it's as simple as being asleep in bed and waking up at random times to my erect penis, which leads to thoughts of masturbation, just because.

I'm sure you are no stranger to some of the scenarios I have just mentioned. The crazy thing is that temptations can go even further.

I've always thought to myself that I could live my life in one of four ways:

1. Be single and live promiscuously. I'm young and educated. I'm a hard worker. I have a solid job history and a brand new car to get to my place of employment. Those facts alone could be benefits for women looking to get it in. "You're young and you're not married?!"

Some would definitely err on the side of sowing my royal oats while I still can. Believe me I've thought about it. However, that way of living would not glorify God.

2. Marry some random woman. Marry someone just because she is an option, and not because she is someone I really love. Marry someone because she's available, even though God did not send her to be my wife. Get with a woman just because she's present and not because I have vetted her spiritually. Going this route would mean that this woman would not compliment me in a way beneficial to my calling, and vice versa. In essence, settle. This option would probably lead me to commit adultery down the line because this woman would not be what I want. Better yet, she would not be what I truly need.

3. Be single and live chaste. This is the way to go if you're single. I'll talk about this more in depth in the next chapter.

4. Get married to one wife. Take the time to seek out a woman, court her, marry her, and love her the way Scripture says I should. Have eyes for her only. This is where your desires matter. You should not commit to marrying someone all while lusting after other people. A person must deal with his/her lustful desires prior to marriage. Conquering lust is imperative to

honoring your husband or wife through your actions and in your thoughts. Being devoted to one person requires your mind to be pure and sober. Your thought life should maintain its focus on the one you are married to and not another. Men, the enemy will let you think it is perfectly okay to lust after other women because you're a man and that's what men do. However, this is a lie from the enemy. Jesus declares in Matthew 5 that if you look at a woman with lust, then you have committed adultery. The physical act of adultery is only a manifestation of the thoughts that run through your mind. You must have self control. You have to maintain your focus. Your intentions should be to please the Lord and your spouse. Don't let this culture's way of thinking lead your marriage to its demise. You are more than a conqueror and can overcome lust if you choose to fight it.

THE DESIRE

Lust comes from the Greek word *epithymia* which means a longing (especially for something that is forbidden), concupiscence, and desire. Concupiscence means a strong desire, especially one that is sexual in nature. So now the question becomes, why do we have a strong desire to do sexual things?

On one hand, being raped, molested, or sexually

abused could have awakened the desire for sex. Or sexual desire could be traced back to your friends in middle or high school introducing it to you. Maybe growing up you were surrounded by family members who were having pre-marital sex and the spirit of lust made its way into your heart. There are a number of ways we can stir up lust, aside from the examples mentioned here. To make a long story short, the desire for sex begins within.

Now to be fair, sex is not a bad thing. God designed sex to be enjoyed within the context of marriage. It's the enemy that makes a sacred thing such as sex perverse. He has thrown the desire for sex in your face so that you don't remain a virgin. If you've lost your virginity, then Satan wants you to keep having sex, and to fulfill every sexual desire you have. He has done a great job of putting sexual desire at the forefront of our minds to distract us as we live our daily lives through television, movies, radio, social media, magazines, friends, family, and the internet.

The longing for love, companionship, and marriage gets distorted by our sexual desires. For example, let's say you meet someone who is attractive. You start getting to know that person through having conversations, going on dates, and hanging out. Then because you're attracted to this person, at some point the desire for more creeps in. You may love the person, yes, but you still want more. It's no longer just wanting to spend every waking moment with him or her. You don't just love the way he or she talks and thinks, or admire his or her style of dress. Not only is your infatuation and love for this person growing but you want to show him or her how you really feel. You want sex. The sparkle in her eyes captivates you. His strong arms and broad shoulders has you undressing him with your eyes. The thoughts of his body in between yours excites you and causes you to send that text with the "wyd," line. The desire to run your fingers through her hair as her hands gently claw your back compels you to want to make that fantasy a reality.

Everything is permissible but not all things are beneficial (1 Corinthians 10:23). Although strong sexual desires are natural, it is not always beneficial for you to act on them. In a culture that permits sex, staying focused on Christ and doing the right thing by not having sex before marriage is not the easiest thing to accomplish. Remaining prayerful and continuing to read & study the Word are two helpful ways to assist in overcoming sexual desire. When temptation presents itself to you, take the way of escape given to you. There is always a way out. Don't let anyone pressure you into losing your virginity or breaking your celibacy. He or she may say they love you but that could just be hormones talking. He or she may just be saying what they know you want to hear just to appeal to your sexual desires. Before you know it, he or she has you wrapped around their finger like a snake wrapped around a tree limb. Ladies, don't let a man sweet talk his way in between your legs because he'll cause a schism between you and God. Men, don't let a woman seduce her way into your bed either because there will be a divide between you and God just the same.

Any relationship that leads you to sin does not glorify God. If a woman loves the Lord and lives for Him, she should not lead you to her bedroom. The same goes for men. Godly relationships should help you fulfill God's will, not lead you to live in sin.

The culture we live in also thinks it's acceptable to live together if you're in a relationship. For many people, this is the next step after dating someone exclusively for a while. From a financial perspective you can split all the bills 50/50. Living together supposedly helps you get closer to each other. Men, you can see what she looks like in the morning. Ladies, you can make him dinner when he gets home from work. So what's the problem? Living together will take the relationship to the next level before the man pops the question.

The thought crosses your mind that this isn't right, we're supposed to be Christians. Man this really doesn't honor God but it feels so good. You continue on living with her and you've just had sex for the first time. As the days progress, your entire thought life has been turned upside down. Thoughts of conviction, lust, guilt, shame, excitement, passion all rolled into one giant chaotic state of thinking. What have we done? You ask. Living together was the next best thing. That's what we were advised to do by everyone we asked. Even the pastor said it was the wise thing to do. You could save money all while getting to know each other better. You did not know that the sexual desire was there. That the longing for her body pressed against yours was there all along.

Living together creates the right set of circumstances and pressure, and sex is usually the final result. Everyone that you listen to, including yourself, has led you to this point. The only person you would have failed to listen to is God. If you would have listened to God, He would have told you that he or she wasn't right for you.

The desire for sex has led many people into situations where things are ok for a little while, until the pressure builds and things begin to break down. Pressure of your natural desire for sex. Peer pressure from your friends to take things to the next level with said girlfriend/boyfriend. Pressure from society telling you that premarital sex is perfectly normal for a person your age. What happens when the relationship then suddenly turns sour because of the mutual decision to have sex? One day something changes, and they no longer look at the person the same. Most people who live together soon lose the sparkle in their eyes that fades into darkness. Their significant other can quickly be reduced to a sex pet.

When people live together they take on the benefits and responsibilities of married life, but without the anchoring weight of commitment. In many people's minds they are married just without the title and other people view them the same way. The man may pay every bill on time and gives the woman money to get her hair and nails done. Their families may get along, with who they expect will be their future son or daughter in-law. They may even go as far as alternating holidays like Christmas with the other's family. It seems like the perfect life. However, no matter how much of a great dream this may be, God did not create us to live like this. God created us to experience real intimacy which can only be experienced through the lifelong commitment of marriage.

Unbelievers aren't the only ones who live that way. Many people who say they are Christians live like that too. Maybe you're one of those people. You're living with your significant other. And no matter how much you've told yourself that one day you two will get married, it's clear that there is no rush, because you two are still not married. Maybe you two even got down on your knees to pray about moving in together. And even though you never got an answer from God to move in together or even to be with this person, you still acted. You moved in together, and maybe after putting up some resistance one day you caved in to your desires and had sex. Maybe you're living just like the rest of your friends and family, and maybe you followed their ill-advised suggestions. Your identity is wrapped up inside of what the culture says, rather than in Christ. If this is you, then yes you may have failed to look at how Scripture instructed you to live. Follow the way the Scriptures say to live and make the decision to no longer live out this lie of "shacking up" today.

GOING THE OTHER WAY
Oftentimes people search for a deeper meaning in life. Society, coupled with family, friends, and the system, advises us to go to college. Then, after graduation you are expected to get a good paying job, get married, and have

kids. That is living out the American dream. So many of us look for deeper meaning, and a sense of belonging in education, hobbies, the family business, relationships, and sometimes addictions.

As we go through life in search of meaning, some form of the following questions come to mind: Who am I? Where do I come from? What makes me, me? Why am I here? Some people attempt to answer these questions from the point of their sexual orientation. Declaring that you are gay, lesbian, or transgender in this day and age is slowly becoming the norm. However, no matter how popular it may be, that way of living is not normal. After all, marriages and relationships between men and women have existed since the beginning of time. In years past, it was frowned upon for a person to come forward and say he or she was gay. However, being gay is the way many people have chosen to live. Many people profess that their gay lifestyle is simply a truth that they choose to live out. "This is my truth," they declare.

In the book of Genesis, Satan caused Eve to question the command given by God to not eat from the tree of the knowledge of good and evil. Eve reasoned with the devil and within herself, and did what was contrary to the commandment given to her by God. In this same manner, the enemy has planted a seed within this generation. This seed has blossomed into a full grown tree with poisonous fruit that appeals to the culture. This fruit has been eaten, and people are being fed by the father of lies (John 8:44). You may wonder if this can be proven, but the current state of the culture makes this evident. Same sex marriage is now legal in all 50 states. Even my native country, Canada is an advocate for same sex marriage. Churches now have openly gay pastors and congregations. Even former President Barack Obama recanted his stance on marriage, and became a proponent for same sex marriage early on in his presidency. American culture has shifted from marriage between and a man and a woman being the traditional way of building a family. Same sex homes/families are being built across the world and the culture is adapting to such changes.

Being gay could be a clear choice that someone makes. This choice may come from years of struggling with the choice to be gay or not early on in life. If you're a man, being attracted to another man is what you like. That attraction may come from being exposed to the same sex, sexually speaking, during the adolescent years of one's life. The seed of attraction to the same sex may have been planted by the enemy through different family members' same sex relationships. Others may claim to be born gay and that they cannot change how they feel towards the same sex.

These illustrations I've just described may be some ways being gay becomes a reality for some. The way one chooses to live is a lifestyle of living out your truth as people say today. That is what's pushed in today's society, to live how you want to live. To live within the reality of one's truth based on their sexual orientation. You should be able to live out your truth free from the restrictions of anyone's opinions. You should be able to have sex with whom you want to have sex with, right? "It's the 21st century, get with the times," you may say. "Progress is needed for a better America to emerge," you may argue. The question is, what lie has Satan or his angels (Revelation 12:7-9) told you to cause you to identify as gay or lesbian? Is living your truth simply by deciding to be gay another lie the enemy has told people?

As I've mentioned previously, people dismiss any argument against their lifestyle by saying "this is my truth." "I was born this way," they sing, and they have a band of people that love them for who they think they are. But just because a person has endorsed one's way of living and approved their choices, does not make a thing right in the eyes of God.

I have never been more keen on living by the Scriptures, than I am right now at this point in my life. People present their opinions to others constantly. There is nothing wrong with people having opinions about what they think is right or wrong. Everyone is entitled to their own opinion. However, it is clear that people seek approval based on the validation of those opinions. They seek reassurance from those they look up to. "If so and so says it's cool, then I'm good. I must be living right." Counsel and wisdom is important to seek out. But what if that counsel and wisdom does not come from God? That is where the danger comes in.

"Now the Spirit speaketh expressly, that in the latter times some shall depart from the faith, giving

heed to seducing spirits, and doctrines of devils; speaking lies in hypocrisy; having their conscience seared with a hot iron...."

—1 Timothy 4:1-2 (KJV)

Many people who attend church have left the faith. They no longer subscribe to what they used to believe based on the choices they've made. They've listened to the lies spoken in their ears and as a result live out a lie. They have been seduced by the father of lies and have been taught by demons. They have been taught that homosexuality is okay, and that God loves them even though they are attracted to the same sex. Let me be clear, homosexuality is wrong. It is clearly outlined in Scripture that homosexuality is not the right way to live. (Romans 1:22-28; Leviticus 18:22,1 Corinthians 6:9; Leviticus 20:13) To the world, homosexuality is perfectly fine, but God sees things differently. "God still loves me," people may say. Yes, but does He approve of what you do? You see the only opinion that really matters is God's. Does HE truly approve of the way you live? He is the person that created you and knows why you exist. He designed you and created you for a specific purpose.

Unfortunately, many people have given in to their relative truth and desires. In advocating their truth they have failed to submit themselves to living out The Truth (John 14:6). These desires have turned into sin, and it has become full grown and now leads to death (James 1:15). This open, but dark, way of living has led to the spiritual death of so many. The enemy may tell you like he's told me in the past, "Well you don't have to worry about getting someone pregnant. You don't have to deal with the emotions of a woman. You can be free to be with whoever you want to be with because this is the land of the free and home of the brave. You're young, do what makes you happy. You're single, attractive and you only live once so why not try it? No one will know about it..." Sure, a person can hide their sin from family, friends, co-workers, and classmates, but they can't hide from God.

> *"The eyes of the Lord are in every place, beholding the evil and the good."*
> —Proverbs 15:3 (KJV)

So if I know that God is always watching me, why sin deliberately? He is watching my every move, knowing where I go and who I talk to.

> *"For the ways of man are before the eyes of the Lord, and he pondereth all his goings."*
> —Proverbs 5:21 (KJV)

My ways are always before the Lord. He ponders, or thinks, about what I do very carefully. He thinks about why we choose to sin or walk upright before Him. He thinks about why some believers choose to fornicate right before they go out to preach. He wonders why men have decided to forsake what's natural to pursue an unnatural passion.

Since God is watching me and I don't want to displease

him, I must do what is right. My beliefs, and the Christ I represent (me being an ordained minister and all), won't allow me to live life as a gay man. My family and what they stand for won't allow me to cross the line from being straight to being gay. My four young brothers and other (young) people who look up to me, will have me think twice before I make certain decisions. The thought of my future wife and children stop me dead in my tracks. I listen to the Scriptures for what not to do. The constant reminders from the Holy Spirit to do what's right, keep me enduring through the struggle of lust and homosexuality. Trust me when I tell you, my thoughts have run aimlessly into thinking about living as a gay man but these reasons alone won't let me go that way. It isn't acceptable to live the way the flesh says I should live, but it is right to live life the Way GOD wants me to live.

To be gay in this day and age is quite normal even among people who claim to be believers. People profess to be wise regarding progress, forward movement, and changing with the times. The debate about gay marriage and the right to be gay may be deemed a social issue by some, but at its core it is a deeply rooted spiritual problem. It is a result of people believing what they want to believe and doing what they want to do:

> *"...God gave them over in the lusts of their hearts to impurity, so that their bodies would be dishonored among them. For they exchanged the truth of God for a lie, and worshiped and served the*

creature rather than the Creator, who is blessed forever. Amen. For this reason God gave them over to degrading passions (and vile--very bad or unpleasant affections); for their women exchanged the natural function for that which is unnatural, and in the same way men abandoned the natural function of the woman and burned in their desire toward one another, men with men committing indecent acts and receiving in their own persons the due penalty of their error."

      —Romans 1:24-27 (NAS, Emphasis Added)

God has given us all freewill, which means we can live exactly how we want to live. In the verses that precede the Romans 1:24-27 passage, it is clear that the Apostle Paul is addressing ungodly and unrighteous men (Romans 1:18-19). Paul speaks to how these men suppress the truth in unrighteousness because that which is known about God is evident within them because God has made it known to them in their hearts (conscience). How is it that men and women know the truth but choose to bury it within what they do? What is known about God and what He expects of you have been made evident inside you already. There is no excuse for you to live unrighteously because the truth has been made known to you. However, many people choose to bury the truth of God with what they do behind closed doors. In doing so they choose to exchange the truth about God for a lie. A lie that looks like a good cause. A lie that leads you to believe that what you're doing is right because of the way you feel. A lie that tells you to go with your gut, rather than go with God. A lie that tells you to follow your heart, without mentioning that the heart is desperately wicked (Jeremiah 17:9). A lie that tells you to shut out those who don't agree with you because you think they don't love you. A lie that feeds off of the friends who say you're right and who offer you their support.

Many people think they are wise by accepting the cause of the LGBTQ community, and progressive sexuality by sleeping with men and/or women outside of God's definition of marriage. But the truth is this has only gotten them further away from God (Isaiah 59:2). If you're such a person then let me warn you that you are going to be given over to impurity and the lusts of your heart, by doing with your body what you see fit, and not what God wants for you. All because you think you are wise. You're exchanging the glory of God for the fool's gold of the culture. The culture says, "Love who you want to love. Have sex with who you want to have sex with. Live. Be free and be happy to be with who you want to be with." But what happens when you've done all there is to do only to find that you are still unhappy? That you still feel unfulfilled? When you still don't see a point to life? What happens when you identify more with the community that's embraced you, than with the God who's created you?

It's a sad story that plays out for many people. They live how they want to live. Then one day they decide to get tested. They find out that they're HIV positive, some even discover that they have full blown AIDS. Some women are now past the age of child bearing and can't have kids, even though once upon a time they wanted to. Now they can't because they've wasted reproductive life being a lesbian. Could this be the due penalty of their errors? Could this be the end of living free and living the way society tells you to live?

Now what amazes me is that the Bible says that in the church even the very elect shall fall away (Matthew 24:24). Believers are not teaching their gay neighbors that the way they are living is wrong. How is this? God requires holy living (1 Peter 1:16). Doesn't He?

I was having a discussion with a good friend of mine. I mentioned that the spirit of homosexuality is such a strong spirit to shake because we are dealing with a spiritual matter (Ephesians 6:12). People believe that a man liking another man is perfectly okay. And that living unnaturally is normal because of the lies they have been told. What baffles me is that many of the people who are living a homosexual lifestyle believe that it is a right way to live.

"The coming of the lawless one will be in accordance with how Satan works. He will use all sorts of displays of power through signs and wonders that serve the lie, and all the ways that wickedness deceives those who are perishing. They perish because they refused to love the truth and so be saved. For this reason God sends them a powerful delusion so that they will believe the lie and so that all will be condemned who have not believed the truth but have delighted in wickedness."
—2 Thessalonians 2:9-12 NIV

Today, when a believer presents the truth of God to an unbeliever, or someone in sin, it comes across as a form of hatred. Yet it is a believer's job to not only declare the Gospel with their mouths, but also by the way they live. Those who live in sin perish because they refuse to love the truth. Not their truth but THE TRUTH. The Truth that comes from God-breathed Scripture, and not from their opinions! God sent a powerful delusion of homosexuality, and people believe it. These souls won't be saved all because they chose not to fall in love with the truth that has the power to save them from hell. They would rather love the man or woman they are having sex with and live out a lie, instead of loving the truth! That's a dangerous way to live.

If God is prompting you to give up this way of living, it is imperative that you listen to Him. God has been speaking to me in different ways and I seek to embrace His words of encouragement. In this life, I have to be obedient to what the Scriptures say. It does not matter how I feel, or what my flesh wants. I refuse to live out a lie because my body wants me to. I must honor God with my body because that is what He requires (1 Corinthians 6:20). God loves you but He requires that you live a certain way. We must live a life that is led by the Spirit of God, and not by the spirit of the culture. You have to align the way you live with Scripture because God is pleased with life being lived THAT WAY. It's okay to follow Jesus and not popular culture. Jesus is the true difference maker, and He can change your heart and mind if you let Him.

IMAGES

On one hand pornography remains something that some people secretly engage with. However, in some circles, pornography has become something that is widely accepted. I was introduced to pornography in high school. Since then I have struggled with it on and off.

The illusion that pornography creates has caused many hearts to be separated from God. This sex-infused industry has caused many marriages to crumble. The porn industry is driven by money and wickedness, and causes the men and women who are filmed to seek purpose in sin. The meaning of life withers away for these people with every orgasm they fake or experience. There is no telling how many young men and women have been forced or manipulated into becoming an adult film actor or actress or have done so of their own free will. What these actors, actresses and stars have had to endure and have been forced to embrace has come at the expense of another. Some of them may be forced to believe that this is their only source of making an income. These men and women have their bodies reduced to just being an object of pleasure and a money-making product.

I cannot speak much from the perspective of an adult film star, however I have been on the receiving end of their work. I once believed Satan's lie that watching porn was to my benefit. But that is not the case. In fact, watching porn only gives a hand to a porn star's spiritual demise. I only know what it feels like to give my body away in theory. However, these exploited men and women are forced to know what it feels like to give their body away every time they go to work. Sex is what they do for a living.

The word fornication comes from the Greek word porneia, meaning illicit sexual intercourse. Unfortunately, this way of living has become many people's source of income, and all the while they are participating in sin. As believers, if we watch others fornicate we are participating in the sin and are also trapped into believing a lie. We may believe that watching pornography gives us what we crave, a human touch. Sex itself. The love that we didn't see growing up. Or even Love Himself (1 John 4:8).

I asked a married friend of mine why he watched pornography. His response was that he watched it because with pornography he didn't have to do the work of romancing and initiating foreplay to have an orgasm, the way he would have to if he was having sex with his wife. His response gives insight into why a lot of people watch pornography: they can experience orgasm and skip the work it takes to be intimate with their spouse. How wrong is this? Very wrong. The husband lusts in his heart for another woman, thus committing adultery (Matthew 5:28). He also watches others fornicate (pornography). Then, more than likely, this man masturbates to get an orgasm because his wife is not there for him to have sex with.

Watching pornography creates a false sense of intimacy. The intimacy people cannot get because they aren't married, or maybe they are married but their spouses are not around, so they think they can get it through watching porn. This way of thinking is not healthy for our marriages, minds, children, or spiritual well being. We must come to the realization of how wrong pornography is. The void we think it fills only causes us to move further away from God, and closer to idolatry.

SELF PLEASURE

Masturbation is something that I struggled with for a very long time. I was introduced to it at a young age through the sexual abuse I endured. There was a time where I had done it so much it became normal to me. The lie I was told was that masturbation is a common act among men and women, and that it was okay to do it. There was no valid reason to justify the act. One lie I've heard constantly about masturbation is this, "I'm not married, so what other way can I get off but to masturbate?" I had a friend once tell me that he would rather masturbate than fornicate. "At least I won't have a kid or get an STD from doing so, so why not touch myself a little bit?"

What we don't realize is that masturbation becomes all about how we can please ourselves. There is no one else involved so we don't have to worry about giving ourselves to another as an act of love. Selfishness is not love (1 Corinthians 13:5). To give love you must think about the well being of others, rather than pleasing yourself.

Not only does masturbation create a false sense of intimacy and promotes selfishness, but it also fails to deliver on what we truly desire. I cannot answer the question of when a spouse will come to fulfill the sexual desire you crave. Sometimes you may sit and wonder, "Well God why am I still single? Why are you torturing me with no sex? Can't she (or he) just show up already?" These are questions I found myself asking.

Refusing to masturbate forces you to have discipline and self-control (Galatians 5:22). Self control helps lead you to die to your flesh everytime you say no to masturbation. Each time you say no, you become victorious, no after no. Don't let the enemy deceive you into thinking this is okay to do, and that no one will know. God will know. He is always watching. Do you feel guilty after masturbating? Then there must be something wrong with the act. I know it's difficult to abstain from, but trust me, the benefit of not doing it supersedes masturbation's temporary pleasure. Stay strong, and hold on to the Solid Rock. You can overcome this, just be willing to die daily. The reward of resisting the devil is far greater than the fleeting pleasure this sin gives (Psalm 19:8,11 NLT).

MAY THE WORD CHANGE YOU...

The reality is that humankind is becoming increasingly, more wicked. As time progresses, things that were once frowned upon are becoming more widely accepted. This is true even amongst believers.

It is sad that I have been influenced by the culture enough to believe the lie. Satan has presented the lie to me leading me to believe that pornography, masturbation, and lust are okay. The truth is, they are not. Believers who practice such sins, as well as fornication and adultery, need to turn away. We all need to repent, for the kingdom is at hand. That is what Jesus preached in Matthew 4:17.

The Greek meaning for the word repent means to think differently. This can be quite challenging for those of us who have been raised to live a certain way. Not only are our children raised to act a certain way, but those actions come from what parents teach their kids. What a parent teaches, comes from what he or she believes. What a person believes can come from church, school, and those within a person's environment. It can also come from the media, the internet, people's opinions, magazines, TV, movies, government, social issues, family, and friends. All of these things can help develop a young child's mind into believing whatever they are fed.

Unfortunately, the things and people that seek to shape the mind, and therefore the way we think and act, have come from the world. Society and all of its mediums have been used to form our minds to live out its creed instead of God's will. Yet, the Scriptures are clear:

> *"Don't copy the behavior and customs of this world, but let God transform you into a new person by changing the way you think. Then you will learn to know God's will for you, which is good and pleasing and perfect."*
> —Romans 12:2(NLT)

Nothing matters more to me now than accomplishing God's will for my life. As I've wrestled with my flesh in relation to my own sexual temptations, God knocks at my door. He reminds me that my heart is what He wants. He wants my body to be presented to him as a living sacrifice, holy, acceptable, and pleasing to Him, which is my spiritual act of worship (Romans 12:1). What I do with my body shows who I'm devoted to (God or myself). What I feed my mind has a direct reflection on what my body does, if self control is not present. If I look at a woman and lust after her in my heart, it's likely that my body will follow the thoughts of my mind. However I have the power to hold those thoughts captive and make them obedient to Christ (2 Corinthians 10:5).

There is direct conviction every time sin crouches at my doorstep. God continues to remind me not to partake in this forbidden fruit, which could be anything sexual. Giving in to sexual sin just breaks down one's spirit and leads to death (James 1:15).

I've never felt so pressed to live out God's will than right now. Even though temptation is present, I can see the darkness attached to it. God's promptings lead me to His presence. They lead me to fall on my knees in surrender. Though I feel dirty, sinful, unrighteous, and wicked at the smallest ounce of sin, nothing is more comforting than the blood of Jesus shed for you and I. There is nothing more precious and peaceful than for God to grace me with His presence even after sin has taken place.

The very thing that can truly keep one's way pure is the Word of God. Scripture carries direction and wisdom for holy living. I can admit that life has at times carried me away from the Truth that should be guiding my every footstep. I have felt so far away from God at times, but then I am reminded that nothing would please God more than to run to Him. I see now more than ever that God's Word truly has the ability to renew and transform my mind. It will totally shatter what previously existed and new life will begin to form.

I pray that as you continue on your journey to sexual purity, that you will allow the words of the Bible to change your way of thinking. Allow God's Word to change how you live. Allow His Spirit to give you a new life that is contrary to the life you used to live. As we head into the final chapters of this book, may God's Word change your life forever and those you come in contact with.

 CHAPTER SEVEN

THE TRUTH

"If we say that we have fellowship with him, and
walk in darkness, we lie, and do not the truth."
— 1 John 1:6 (KJV).

Each one of us must make one of two choices: to walk in darkness or to walk in truth. Throughout the entire year of 2018, Satan and his angels had been on my tail to engage in sexual activity. Some of his attempts were subtle, others were overt. Even something as small as a dirty joke towards me, I believe is still an attack on my sexual purity. I strive to live a pure life, yet still I have had temptation play on my emotions and give me false desires that warred within my members. The wrong that I have engaged in, no matter how big or small, has led me to feelings of guilt, shame, sadness, loneliness, hopelessness, and doubt. The truth that I have been compelled to live out has not been an easy road to walk. I know who God created me to be, but the reality is Satan constantly presents his way to go about living as well. God's way leads to life. Satan's way leads to death. Plain and simple.

It's not enough to simply walk around the earth living any way you want. We need some sort of guidance to assist in godly living. The world presents one way to live. God presents the way we ought to live. We can find God's way in the Bible. The 66 books that compose the Bible tell us exactly how to live a life that is pleasing to the Father. Ladies and gentlemen, living by the words in Scripture will guarantee a life of sexual purity if you choose to be a doer of the Word. Living a life in this manner will come with much rejection. People will think you're weird. Your decision will be unpopular. I can assure you that living the way Scripture tells us to live comes with much peace, freedom, and security in Christ! His way is the only way to go!

THE WAY

> *Jesus saith unto him, I am the way, the truth, and the life: no man cometh unto the Father, but by me.*
> —John 14:6 (KJV)

> *Then said Jesus to those Jews which believed on him, If ye continue in my word, then are ye my disciples indeed: And ye shall know the truth, and the truth shall make you free.*
> —John 8:31-32 (KJV)

The Bible is the first place to go for direction on how to live a life of sexual purity. Living in the Word, as Jesus put it, will cause you to know the truth. That truth will set you free (John 8:32). I am compelled by the Lord to live a life that is pleasing to Him. This has been no easy feat. Man will always have their opinions. Society will put their two cents in. However, if you listen to man and the world but don't consult God, you will end up living a lie. God holds the truth, and it was lived out by His Son Jesus when He was on the earth. Jesus is the Truth, and Scripture has advised us to follow His example (1 Peter 2:21). Following Jesus, and doing what He says, is the only way we can experience a fulfilled life.

A young person asked me recently, "Damien, how have you gone this long without having sex?" The simple answer is I avoided sex. Truthfully, in moments of temptation, I would say, "Girl don't touch me like that. Don't touch me and I won't touch you. If you keep hugging me like that, we're gonna make a baby." However, as I have given the question more thought, one important Scripture comes to mind:

> *"How can a young man keep his way pure? By living according to your word."*
> —Psalm 119:9 (NIV)

I've also abstained from sex because of my fear of God and what is written in the Bible. I knew that if I did what the Bible says, I would remain pure. One of the best ways to avoid having pre-marital sex is to be a doer of the Word, such as "Flee fornication…" (1 Corinthians 6:18). The excuse, "I'm only human," or "Sex is natural," or "God created me with a sex drive," will not work. You can't say,

"Well I'm young, single, attractive, and I'm in the prime of my life. I have to get it in while I still can. I have to sow my royal oats!" While all these things may be true, fornication still is not God's will for the believer.

> "...It is good for a man not to touch a woman. Nevertheless, to avoid fornication, let every man have his own wife, and let every woman have her own husband."
> —1 Corinthians 7:1-2 (KJV)

This sentence is tricky. After all, human touch is something people crave. A hug. A kiss. A simple touch on the shoulder. Although the touch of a woman admittedly feels good, one thing has always remained in the back of my mind—the desire to be married. Women never threw themselves at me. I have never had a woman just drop her clothes in front of me and then have something happen. I have not had a real romantic relationship in my adult life, so the opportunity for sex has simply not presented itself to me. Even in instances where I have hit on a girl, or vice versa, I knew that crossing the line was not an option.

Why is crossing the line into unknown territory not an option? The answer is simple. Marriage is the one place where God is alright with two people of the opposite sex having sex. Once I saw that God did not approve of fornication in Scripture, I knew that I could not be foolish enough to pursue it. What I believe does not allow me to go there. The fact of the matter is the Bible outlines clear ways to live a life of sexual purity. Society, family, friends, the world, Satan, and his angels all have their opinion, but none of those entities created me. We cannot live for people's approval. The Lord's approval and validation is all we need to live out God's will.

> *"For do I now persuade men, or God? or do I seek to please men? for if I yet pleased men, I should not be the servant of Christ."*
> —Galatians 1:10 (KJV)

I have to serve God in every way possible. He has clearly worded in Scripture how we are supposed to conduct ourselves when it comes to sex. The Bible should be our guide to daily living. Without Scripture, we cannot successfully overcome sexual immorality. I pray that the pages of this book help you on your own journey to sexual purity.

WHAT THE BIBLE SAYS ABOUT SEX

> *"...Now the body is not for fornication, but for the Lord; and the Lord for the body."*
> —1 Corinthians 6:13 (KJV)

First thing's first. Your body does not belong to you, it belongs to the Lord. This verse eludes to the same principle found in Romans 12:2, presenting ourselves as a living sacrifice. Everything about what you do with your body should be for the Lord.

"Know ye not that your bodies are members of Christ? Shall I then take the members of Christ, and make them the members of an harlot? God forbid."
—1 Corinthians 6:15 (KJV)

Let's be honest. Because I don't have a girlfriend, the temptation to have pre-marital sex is not as strong. Even though I am single, I am reminded that I can't just have sex with anyone who crosses my path. Although the option is always there, I regularly make the choice to not let my body succumb to its nature. I am young, handsome, and educated. I have a place of my own and a nice car. People may say, "Hey. YOLO. You only live once. You're young, live a little. What happens if you die tomorrow? Do you want to die a virgin?" Well, what happens if I don't? Some people may even go as far as saying, "Well Jesus isn't real," or "Jesus was human too, I bet He had sex with Mary or Martha or some other fine woman." People can say a number of things to convince you that it is okay to do as you please. They argue, "You're in the prime of your life. Having sex should be apart of your life. It's okay to do it right now." But says who? Says your friends? Says some magazine article? Says the culture? Says you?

But what if Jesus is real? What if everything in Scripture is what we should follow? What if there is a reward for my faithfulness as a virgin? My body belongs to Christ. I cannot take my body and indulge in sexual exploits. I can't just find a woman that I'm attracted to, and then have my way with her. Yes, technically I could if she allowed me to, but it would not be beneficial to my walk with God. He would not approve of such actions.

I'm not going to lie. Sometimes I sit and wonder if I will ever get married. My mind does wander into lustful thoughts. I do wonder if I will ever get married, and have children, and build a family with a wife God provides. But until that day comes, I must remain as I am, serving the Lord (1 Corinthians 7:20, 27). Again, I say, this is no easy feat. Jealousy and envy have reared their ugly heads in my heart. However, I am learning how to be content with my singleness in this season. I am pushing aside the temptation to juxtapose my life with others, and embracing being at peace with who I am. I'm becoming more and more comfortable in my own skin. I am finally beginning to experience the reward and security that avoiding pre-marital sex brings.

A relationship has enough challenges as it is, but when you add pre-marital sex to a relationship I'm sure it only makes matters worse. Thank God, I don't have that problem right now! An unmarried man is concerned about the Lord's affairs—how he can please the Lord (1 Corinthians 7:32). This has been an area of intense focus for me lately. Nothing matters to me more in this season than walking out the calling of God on my life, and to remain in His will. The desire to carry out God's will has become more intense because I realize that there is nothing more important. Nothing should matter more to the believer than to preach the Gospel through their respective gift and calling.

Pre-marital sex and everything related to it, is just

designed to throw you off course. Pre-marital sex puts the focus on you and everything you want, rather than on God, which is where it should be. Fornication fixes your eye on the woman or man you have sex with, and takes your eyes off of the Lord. Pre-marital sex leads you to idolatry, it leads you to intentionally worship another god, instead of submitting your body to its Creator — the Lord.

IT'S DEEPER THAN JUST NOT HAVING SEX

"What? know ye not that your body is the temple of the Holy Spirit which is in you, which ye have of God, and ye are not your own? For ye are bought with a price; therefore glorify God in your body, and in your spirit, which are God's."
—1 Corinthians 6:19-20

The word "temple" in the Greek is *naio*, which can be translated "to dwell." With this in mind, it is clear that your body, and mine, is a place where the Holy Spirit lives. Who is the Holy Spirit? The Holy Spirit is the person who will guide us into all truth, according to John 16:13. Holy Spirit will remind us of Jesus' teachings, and teach us how to live. Holy Spirit speaks to us and tells us what He hears from the Father, and He also shows us things to come (John 16:13).

The Holy Spirit will also reprove the world of sin, of righteousness, and of judgment (John 16:8). The word reprove in the Greek form can be translated to mean "convict or convince." The thing about us humans is that oftentimes we do not want to take responsibility for our actions. When we are presented with a way that is contrary to what we want to do, we tend to push it away. If Truth comes into your picture frame, and shows you that the image you are portraying is incorrect, you would likely disagree. Satan wants you to believe that your way is right. But the Holy Spirit will convict you of your sin and tell you when you are wrong.

The line between Satan's deception and the Truth of God is your faith. Can you believe that a sinless Man came to the earth to save you from hell? Will you believe that He died on the cross for your sins so that you could live with His Father in eternity? Will you believe that the Holy Spirit was sent to the earth after Christ's ascension to help you live according to the Scriptures? Your faith in all of the above will be the defining moment between you giving in to sexual immorality or staying away from it and reigning over sexual temptation.

God's command to save sex until marriage is not a rule meant to restrict you (1 Corinthians 7:35). God created your body. He created your body to glorify Him, even before your spouse comes along. Then, as you live in obedience to Him, He will present your wife or husband to you. At that point your bodies will belong to each other (1 Corinthians 7:4). However, your body will still be the temple of God. Thus, while you are single your entire focus should be on honoring God with your body. It's not just a matter of abstaining from sex, because unbelievers can do that too. The difference is the reason behind your choice to abstain.

> *1 Thessalonians 4:3-4 declares, "For this is the will of God, even your sanctification, that you should abstain from fornication: That every one of you should know how to possess his vessel in sanctification and honor." (KJV) "It is God's will that you should be sanctified: that you should avoid sexual immorality; that each of you should learn how to control your own body in a way that is holy and honorable..." (NIV)*

The word sanctification in Greek is *hagiasmos*, which can be translated purification, or the state of purity. A second meaning, or deeper translation, is to make holy, or to purify, or to separate for special use. God desires that you save yourself for marriage so that you remain pure and set apart for His use as you wait on marriage. The purpose of abstaining from fornication is to show your devotion to God by devoting your body to Him. In doing so, you honor God and the body He has given you. A body that is used by God is of more value than a body that is abused by multiple people. Do the people you have had sex with really value you? If they saw your worth the way God does, they would have refrained from having sex with you until the two of you were united in holy matrimony. That is honor. Honoring a woman by taking her hand in marriage requires respect on the part of the man. Marriage requires a man to look at Scripture and realize that he can't have sex with this woman unless he marries her, to do otherwise would be disrespectful in the eyes of God. The man and the woman should both look at Scripture and say, "It's God's best for both us to wait until we're married to have sex." This decision honors God.

The reason why I have not had sex yet is because I have chosen not to. Over the years I have come to realize that sex before marriage is not something I am supposed to be doing with my body as a disciple of Christ. Jesus lived His life on earth without ever having sex so surely I can abstain until God looks down from heaven and says I'm ready to be married (Genesis 2:18).

Today young people are taught to refrain from having sex too early because they could get an STD or end up with an unplanned pregnancy. What they are not taught are the spiritual ramifications that come with having premarital sex. The emotional, mental, and sometimes physical consequences that fornication brings on a person's life. The youth are not being taught how to possess their bodies in purity and honor before the Lord.

A good friend of mine reminded me that there is so much value in remaining a virgin. I confess there are times when I have envied other people's relationships and marriages because of what it represents. I have even envied ungodly relationships and marriages because I knew that they were having sex. I have often been sad and discouraged, wondering why God has not given me a wife yet. But then I am reminded of how pure Jesus was on earth. I am reminded of what the Bible says about walking uprightly before the

Lord. I am reminded of how much influence Jesus has had on my life and what that has meant to me. I also look at people around me, people who look up to me, many of them young males. I am reminded that I have to continue as I am because people are watching me. And many of those same people want to see a godly example of a man. So I keep pushing myself. I remind myself that what I am doing is bigger than me, it's for my generation.

WHY DOES SEX EXIST?

For those of you reading this book, we all know, or can imagine, how pleasurable sex is. Sex provides an opportunity for you to show your spouse how much you love them in a physical way. Sex also exists for one other purpose: to produce children.

> *"So God created man in his own image, in the image of God created he him; male and female created he them. And God blessed them, and God said unto them, 'Be fruitful, and multiply, and replenish the earth, and subdue it: and have dominion over the fish of the sea, and over the fowl of the air, and over every living thing that moveth upon the earth.'"*
> —Genesis 1:27-28 (KJV)

I love the fact that this verse tells us we were created in the image of God. We were created to be a reflection of Him. I would like to take it a step further and remind us that we were created to be like Jesus, made to follow in His footsteps (1 Peter 12:21). We were created to endure temptation and to overcome it (1 Corinthians 10:13). We were created to suffer for righteousness and live a life that is pleasing to the Father.

With that being said, the Genesis text teaches us that we were created to be fruitful, to multiply, and to replenish the earth. This requires a man and a woman to come together and create life alongside God's creative, omnipotent abilities. Isn't that so amazing? Everything about this Scripture just says life to me. The fact that a man and a woman can come together and create a child is just beautiful to me. After all the Scripture declares that:

> *"Lo, children are a heritage of the Lord and the fruit*
> *of the womb is his reward."*
> —Psalm 127:3 (KJV)

The word reward in Hebrew is *sakar,* and it can be translated "payment of contract". Children are indeed the fruit that comes from the womb (Psalm 127:3). I would like to think that they are the payment God provides because of the marriage covenant between a man and a woman. God rewards his people when things are done His way; I truly believe that.

The word multiply in Hebrew is *raba,* which means to increase in whatever manner. Now, today having multiple children has its financial restraints. Moreover, having children carries an emotional, mental, and physical weight on parents as well. Still, having children is a natural benefit to sex, so why not have as many children as the Lord allows! Of course, spouses will have plenty of conversations about this subject and weigh the options as it relates to their personal lives.

The word replenish in Hebrew is *mala*, which can be translated to mean male or to fill. I would like to think that this word applies to children as well. God desires a godly seed (Malachi 2:15). The word replenish also means consecrate in Hebrew. God wants us to fill and consecrate the earth (make it holy or set apart) with holy offspring. We have to raise children who are set apart to do the work of the Lord and to carry out His will. We have to raise children who will be doers of the Word and not just hearers of the Word. We have to raise up a generation who have knowledge of the Scriptures and who know who God is! Unfortunately, I am afraid that we're living in a time where people have no clue of who God is. We are witnessing a generation who does not understand or know the God that their parents serve.

It is easy my friends, to be in a romantic relationship with the same sex. You live with your partner. You travel and enjoy life. But the truth is a man cannot go home to another man and conceive children naturally. People can spend thousands of dollars and find a surrogate, but a man cannot have a child. If two women are in a relationship they can go to a sperm donor and spend a large sum of money for in vitro fertilization. However, it takes the sperm of a man to make this possible. These are all popular options for same sex couples to have children, but none of them are natural. A same sex couple can also adopt a child. However, marriage between a man and a woman is the way God intended for children to be brought into this world.

Now I do understand that there are heterosexual couples who go through hard times and who may be unable to conceive on their own. I confess, I do not understand why this happens. I don't have the answer to the reason behind a low sperm count or a barren womb. I do not have the answer to other fertility problems that heterosexual couples face today. I also understand that heterosexual couples can have children by adoption, fostering or surrogacy. This is perfectly ok! All I know is what God has presented to us in Scripture about how to create children. I pray that God grants those married couples who have trouble bearing children the family they desire. After all, I want to find a wife and have children one day.

THROWING AWAY
YOUR CHANCE TO PRODUCE

> "Then Judah said to Oman, 'Lie with your brother's wife and fulfill your duty to her as a brother-in-law to produce offspring for your brother.' But Onan knew that the offspring would not be his; so whenever he lay with his brother's wife, he spilled his semen on the ground to keep from producing offspring for his brother. What he did was wicked in the Lord's sight; so he put him to death also."
> —Genesis 38:8-10 (NIV)

People who do not desire to have children often find a

way to avoid getting pregnant. There are plenty of birth control options for men and women alike. You may often hear from a man to another: "Man, my pull out game is strong!" But here's the thing: Onan would often pull out because he knew the children produced wouldn't be his, and spill his semen on the ground, and God was not pleased with these actions. God killed Onan as a result of his choice.

This story relates to masturbation in the sense that every time a man does so, he spills his semen wherever. This semen is not given the chance to produce children as it should but rather is thrown away and left to die after intercourse. As I have mentioned before, masturbation is something that I've struggled with since my early teenage years. As I began to study Scriptures in my adult life, I came across this one. Once I saw this Scripture, I knew that my actions were just as wrong as Onan's. Recently, I received another revelation behind these common acts: I've been wasting my seed. What is meant to produce fruit in the womb, does not produce anything. Sperm can only carry out its purpose within a woman's womb. Semen is meant to leave a man's body, enter the womb of a woman, find the egg, and ultimately produce a child. Masturbation does not please God, and it does not carry out God's will. Children will never result from masturbation. Masturbation will never be able to carry out God's creative purpose for sex, or help you to be fruitful, multiply, or replenish the earth.

I must be found faithful with what God has given me. Being a faithful steward over what God gives me does not just apply to money. It also applies to the gifts I have. It applies to everything that God has given me including my seed. It applies to my body and honoring God with it. In this season of my life, if I am faithful over the small, then surely God will make me ruler over many things (Matthew 25:21). I have to be faithful now in preparation for what is to come: marriage and children!

FREE TO LIVE

Hopefully this chapter helped shed some light on what the Bible says about sexual purity. The Scriptures are clear that the truth will set you free (John 8:32)! The Bible has made me feel quite secure and confident in the way I live. The Bible should be every Christian's life line because it shows us how to live. Doing things God's Way gives me so much confidence. I know, trust, and believe that God is in this. There is no other way to live. There is no other way to live a life free of Satan's grasp than to do what the Scriptures advise. When temptation creeps at the door of your heart, resist the devil and he will flee (James 4:7). When temptation lurks at my doorstep, I am reminded that I must master sin, as God admonished Cain in Genesis 4:7. Though fornication, homosexuality, and all things evil desire to have me, I must master it! Although I am pressed on every side to do whatever I want, just because I can, I am reminded that there is life in doing things God's way. There is a possible reward coming if I choose to do right. That reward could come through marriage here on earth or in heaven while living with God forever. I pray for both one day. Until those days come, I walk in faith because I am free to live. I am free to live exactly the way God intended for me to live, by following the Scriptures.

May you be blessed as you live out the Truth! May this same Truth keep you living a life of sexual purity to please the Father. May others see that you live for God and that you choose to reign over sexual immorality by listening to, following, and living out His Truth.

 CHAPTER EIGHT

THE CULMINATION

"Blessed are the pure in heart: for they shall see GOD."
—Matthew 5:8 (KJV)

Recently, this Scripture gave me new revelation. The word blessed in Greek is *makarios* and can also be translated to mean: to be well off, fortunate, or happy. This Scripture provides such hope! Peace radiates from its words. Blessed are the pure in heart for they shall see GOD. They may not see marriage. They may not receive an award. They will not have people's approval. But they will see God. Plain and simple. Whenever we realize that living in purity will get us untainted access to God, we will be at peace. We can live with an eternal security, knowing that we will spend eternity with Him. Moreover, we will know that Holy Spirit is with us, and His presence goes before us. God's presence provides a deep sense of security, and there's unexplainable peace that comes from Heaven. This divine peace only resides in God's eternal dwelling. No pornographic website, no man, no woman, and no amount of self pleasure can provide the peace of mind that living for God can. Following Jesus and His way will give you favor; whereas, sin only leads to a dead end.

> *"Who can ascend into the hill of the Lord? Or who shall stand in his holy place?"*
> —Psalm 24:3 (KJV)

These are two critical questions that the Psalmist asks. The next verse (Psalm 24:4) provides the answer: He that hath clean hands, and a pure heart. There is a direct correlation between standing in God's presence and purity. We are graced to be in God's presence. We do not only honor God by praising His name when we enter a special room, we honor Him by how we live before we enter that sacred place. We have to watch what we do with our hands. We have to guard our heart (Proverbs 4:23) and watch over what we allow to get inside of it.

All of these things encompass being in God's presence and in His sanctuary (Psalm 96:6). Following these instructions can give you the strength you need to live for Him. There is much pressure to get you to succumb to your sexual desires before marriage, and even within marriage. With men or women, and sometimes both, lobbying to get your attention to have sex with them, sexual purity can be hard to maintain if you are not taking the necessary precautions. Scripture will keep you when nothing else can.

There have been times where I have gotten away from studying the Word. Yet every time I am at my wits end, and

I open the Bible, I receive the Help I need to keep going. With the easy accessibility the internet provides pornographic content is right at your fingertips, and can be in your direct line of sight at the click of a button. With that being said, we should make the Word of God just as accessible. Whether it's downloading the Bible App on to your smart device. I've even downloaded the God Over Porn App as well as the BLOCKADE App. The former sends me daily notifications with Scripture and quotes that help fight against the struggle with pornography. The BLOCKADE App, blocks me from accessing any website with pornography via the internet.

You could even take your Bible with you wherever you go, and leave it in your car. You can take it with you as you ride public transportation. Making it a point to get up in the morning and read Scripture has helped me out as well. It keeps me on the straight and narrow path God desires to see me on. Getting up out of bed and pushing myself to spend much needed time with God in His Word helps me not to sin against Him (Psalm 119:11). What am I trying to say? Just as pornography is easily accessible, you must make the Bible just as accessible. You must be willing to feed yourself the Scriptures daily (Matt hew 6:11). That way when the desire to watch porn comes knocking at your door, you can shut the door in the enemy's face with the Scriptures quickly!

Be watchful for the triggers that cause you to fall into this area of sexual immorality. Pray against it, so that it won't overtake you. If you know sexy women that walk by are triggers for you to go home and watch porn, then don't look (Job 31:1)! Take the necessary precautions, find someone to help keep you accountable, open the Bible daily, and ask the Holy Spirit to help you overcome this and other forms of sexual immorality. You can do this with the sword of the Spirit in one hand which is the Word of God and the shield of faith in the other (Ephesians 6:16-17). Your faith alone will help extinguish all darts of sexual immorality that the devil tries to throw your way! Do whatever it takes to keep the Scriptures in your line of eye-sight. Images of porn will block your attention from Jesus and from living like, and for, Him. The Bible however will remind you how to live like Him and for Him. Put Scriptures up on the wall of your home through art. Write Scriptures on post it notes and stick them to your mirror in the bathroom. Place the Bible on your nightstand and read it as many times as you're compelled to. MAKE THE BIBLE ACCESSIBLE, so that way it's words remind you of what not to do, and what to do, in staying away from pornography and sexual immorality in general.

As you get older, you will notice that people can start to care less about you. What I mean by that is this, people get caught up in living their own lives. They may stop calling to check in on you. You may hang out with your friends less and less because life begins to take over. Others are seeking to work out their own salvation just as much as you are. With that being said, accountability can be less frequent in the area of sexual purity, as you get older. When this begins to happen, you have to pull on God for strength. You have to say NO. You must have self-control (Galatians 5:23). Pray and refuse to give in. People may tell you to do the opposite of everything I've just written, but believe God. There is a reward on the other side of resisting temptation. HIM. There is strength to be gained from not giving in to the flesh. You can do ALL THINGS through Christ which strengthens you (Philippians 4:13).

Throughout life, we can see certain patterns from our parents that may have tried to manifest themselves in our own lives. Though this may be the case, it does not matter what your parents have done before you. It does not matter if your role models have failed you. I don't care if your pastor was involved in a sexual scandal. Even if all the men in your family are adulterers. You may have been raped, molested, and sexually abused. You could have been involved in sex trafficking, prostitution, and the adult film industry. You still have the power to say no to sexual immorality. You can still choose to maintain a life of sexual purity if you really want to. You have the ability to reign over your sexual desires and impulses, because despite all these things you are MORE THAN A CONQUEROR (Romans 8:37).

I am a living example that you can still live a good life without having premarital sex. You can still have a social life. You can still have a successful career and become a productive member of society. You can still have fun. You can most definitely walk out your calling and do what you love. You can experience true happiness while following Jesus and living like Him. Why? Because you'll be living to please the Father, and not your flesh or other people. Don't give your body away to a man or woman who does not care about you. Don't give your body to people for profit and their personal gain.

Nothing else matters more to God than you living with Him forever. However, in order for that to happen you must believe that His Son Jesus lived and died for you. Believe that He rose again, all for you. Jesus loved you enough to die for you, and conquered death, sin, and the grave so that you could have the victory. Love yourself enough to honor God with your body. Love yourself enough to keep your body for your future husband or wife (if that's God's will for your life). Rest your eyes tonight knowing that your commitment to God through sexual purity does not go unnoticed by Him. Live the rest of your single life knowing that your devotion to God through abstaining from premarital sex is a sure fire way to honor Him.

Yes, today's culture will come to you with strong temptations. And a quick marriage is not the cure to all sexual struggle. There will always be a more beautiful woman who is not your wife or a more handsome man that is not your husband. Marriage is not a quick fix, but when it's Christ-centered it can contain the burning desire for sex because you and your spouse will be able to fill that desire, with each other.

The world may present you with the option to have a relationship with someone of the same sex, but remember God says that is unnatural. When you are single, you could easily go through a string of relationships: sex and all. You could easily have friends with benefits. You could easily explore your sexuality because society says it's part of the typical college experience. Or maybe you just got divorced and society says you're free now. You may be in a mid-life crisis and say to yourself, "Let me find someone who really loves me." You could easily make the excuse, "My ex wife didn't understand me sexually but this new woman rocks my world," or "My ex husband didn't understand my body, but this man's touch is healing me in all the right places." Don't let the enemy feed you these lies. Whether you believe it or not, these same lies will lead you down the path of spiritual destruction. You cannot allow the deception of the enemy to keep you in bondage.

> *It is He that giveth salvation unto kings; who*
> *delivereth David his servant from the hurtful sword.*
> —Psalm 144:10 (KJV)

When you decide to reign over sexual immorality, God will have your back. The word salvation in Hebrew (*tesu a*) means rescue, deliverance, help, safety, and victory. Despite our struggles with sexual immorality in different areas, God can give us the victory. I am living proof. God delivered me from the demonic forces that wanted to destroy my life. And He can do the same for you. We just have to choose to walk in God's freedom and not get caught within the web of sin, which so easily entangles (Hebrews 12:1 NIV).

Personally, this Scripture reminded me that I am a king,

because I am a son of The King. Therefore, as a king I should behave myself accordingly and that includes shunning all things that are sexually immoral. Since I have royalty in my blood, I should conduct myself in a manner that is pleasing to the King. As a king, I have power and authority over everything related to sexual immorality because Christ reigns (Romans 5:17). As Christ—in His obedience to God the Father—died for my sin, I must die to my flesh so that the King in me reigns over sexual immorality. And you should too!

I know dying to our sexual desires is easier said than done. However, it is the way of the transgressor that is hard (Proverbs 13:15) not the way of the believer. Do not make life harder for yourself by giving into your flesh. The truth is giving in and sleeping with that person and having your heartbroken, or catching an STD, or having an unplanned child will make your life significantly harder. Your life will no longer be focused solely on the Lord's affairs. Your focus will change to include either mending your heart, treating your STD, or raising a child because you aroused love before its time (Song of Songs 2:7, 8:4).

This is my heart for you dear reader: May the entire Word of God change your ways and direct your life. May the Word of God keep you in perfect peace and give you victory over sexual sin and over all sin. Allow the Holy Spirit to guide you into all truth. Allow Him to teach you right from wrong. The only thing that can burn away the stench of sexual immorality is the Consuming Fire (Hebrews 12:28). Let Him burn away the years of sexual abuse or sexual perversion or promiscuity or fornication or adultery, of all sexual immorality from your life. If you have fallen in the past, whether knowingly or unknowingly, it's okay, God forgives you (1 John 1:9). Turn away from your sin and sin no more (John 8:11). Be willing to submit to God. Allow the Scriptures to shape the way you live so that you can stand in the midst of a sexually immoral culture (Ephesians 6:14). Stand on the Sure Foundation, the Solid Rock—Jesus Christ.

Jesus did not waver in the way He lived and you must not either. Do not let the ever-changing waves of the culture steer you away from the Father. May God guide you with every step you take. May God remind you of His teachings when sin crouches at your door. May you stand firm on the foundation of Scripture, holding that sword to help you win the fight against the enemy (Ephesians 6:17). May you trust and know that God has your back when you live for Him. Be confident in your stance. Honor God with your body, and know that there is a reward for your faithfulness to Him. Believe the Truth of God and walk out God's will for your life.

You have the power to reign over sexual immorality because the battle is not yours, but the Lord's (2 Chronicles 20:15). The King of Kings defeated sexual immorality when He died on the cross for you and I. Jesus lived a sinless life to show us that it is possible to reign over sexual immorality and all sin. The ability to rule over sexual immorality is in your blood because you were created to subdue and have dominion (Genesis 1:28).

Let this be your reminder as temptation comes from natural and unnatural desires alike. You have dominion. Say it out loud: I reign over sexual immorality because the King living in me reigns over sexual immorality. As a king, or queen, when you say something it is law. The Bible says, you will decree a thing and it shall be established (Job 22:28). The word decree in Hebrew is *gazar* meaning to decide. So if you decide not to have premarital sex, you can establish that in your actions! You have the power and choice to say no to your flesh and yes to The Way the Scriptures say we should live!

May the words from the Bible shed light on how you live. May the Word of God, coupled with your actions and faith, compel you to change. Death and life is in the power of the tongue (Proverbs 18:21), that is how much authority you have as a king and queen, as a son and daughter of the King. Now that the knowledge of how to rule over sexual immorality has been made known to you, it is up to you to walk in the freedom that Truth provides (John 8:32). Trust and believe that though the enemy seems to be winning the battle for the world, Jesus already won the war at the cross. Jesus defeated the enemy once before and He will again, at His second coming. Until that day comes, trust the Lord. Walk in the power of His might! Be strong.

> *Put on the whole armor of God, that ye may be able to stand against the wiles of the enemy. For we wrestle not against flesh and blood, but against principalities, against powers, against the rulers of*

darkness of this world, against spiritual wickedness
(wicked spirits) in high (heavenly) places.
—Ephesians 6:11-12 (KJV)

May your heart and your loins be girded with the belt of truth. When temptation comes your way, say: "Nope! My heart is for the Lord, and my loins are on lock until I get married or until I get to heaven!" Command your thoughts. Remind yourself: "I am a new person in Christ and every [lustful] thought is now brought into captivity to the obedience of Christ (2 Corinthians 10:4-5)." You were created to have victory over sexual immorality so walk in that freedom! You can do it king! You can do it queen! Reign over sexual immorality today!

THE PROMISE REVEALED

"Now to Him who is able to do above and beyond all that we ask or think according to the power that works in us — to Him be glory in the church and in Christ Jesus to all generations, forever and ever. Amen."
—Ephesians 3: 20-21 HCSB

It was the night of August 5th, 2005. I dreamt that my hands were raised and there was what appeared to be golden rays of light all around. I had gold bracelets on both wrists. I also had gold rings on my right and left hands. The ring that was on my left hand however was placed on my wedding finger. Engraved on the ring was the word "BREAKTHROUGH." This dream was my first indication that God had promised me something: marriage.

I've shared my journey from 2005 to 2018 with you up until now, but there is one final leg of the journey yet to be discussed. In August 2018, I traveled to Jamaica for my aunt's funeral. While I was on that trip, I met a girl. She was giving me all the right vibes and I was feeling her too.

I got her number, but at some point throughout the course of that trip, God began to speak to me. He began to tell me that someone else was waiting for me. I had my eyes on one woman, but God was alluding to the fact that I would find my wife VERY soon.

One night, when I returned home to Georgia, I went out to grab a bite to eat. While standing in line to order my food, God began to speak to me. I knew based on what He disclosed to me, that I had to change my actions. I had to let go of the counterfeit, the one I thought was someone I could kick it with, for who God really had for me. Typically in times past, I would know immediately that a girl was not for me. Call it discernment, but I truly leaned on the leading of the Holy Spirit for direction in this regard. I never wanted to be without God's direction, especially when it came to choosing my wife.

God continued to speak to me in my dreams concerning my wife, and I wrote down what He would say. I wrote them down, as a witness so that when God fulfilled His promise of marriage to me, I could go back to the written accounts. God's fulfillment of His promise to me and these dreams would bear witness.

Interestingly enough, I heard God tell me all throughout 2018: "You're going to get married in 2019," but I thought I was just hearing things, and never wrote it down in my journal. Still, I never forgot what I heard. I admit there was a hint of doubt floating through my mind: "Who's getting married? Me? To whom? Where she at Lord?" Come to find out, as of 2018, I had known my wife for 9 years. But it wasn't until August 2018 that it was revealed to me that she would be my wife.

So as history would have it, on Saturday, November 9, 2019 I married Sectrina Danielle Howard (aka Trina) before God, our family and our friends. It was a beautiful ceremony and day. If I could, I would go back and relive that day everyday for the rest of my life.

Now here's the thing, while Trina and I were courting, temptation was at an all time high. I had never made any of those girls from my past my girlfriend, and I only asked Trina because I knew that she would be my wife. There was no need to waste time on anyone else, because God spoke, and I listened. With the others, God didn't say a word. That's what you have to listen for, God's voice and His leading when it comes to choosing your spouse—not your family, or friends but God, and God alone. Because it is God who brings two together in holy matrimony (Mark 10:9).

So let me answer your burning question: Damien did you remain sexless until marriage? EVEN while courting Trina? YES! By the grace of God I did! With God's assistance Trina and I saw through our commitment to not have sex with each other before we were married. And thank God we made it to the altar without doing so. I have to be honest, it was extremely difficult and there were a couple of close calls, but we made it. We only made it because we chose to depend on God to be our strength when we became weak (2 Corinthians 12:9).

In today's day and age, it seems like EVERYONE is having sex, Christians included, and it is accepted. However, this should not be for Ephesians 5:3 declares, "But among you there must not be even a hint of sexual immorality, or of any kind of impurity, or of greed because these are improper for God's holy people."

I was so scared that I'd lose my virginity while courting Trina, so we HAD TO SET BOUNDARIES! I'm not going to pretend, those close calls happened when we did not maintain the boundaries we set for one another.

If you are courting your future spouse or even just dating anyone for that matter, you must set boundaries. Don't be alone with each other at home. Don't kiss that spot that you know will get him or her sexually aroused. When the date is over, do not go up to her apartment or go inside his house. Stay outside, say goodnight and then and GO HOME. Steal away to your prayer closet regularly, and eat the Word of God daily. Watch and pray, so that you won't even enter the temptation to have sex. You must make up in your mind that you both will honor God and each other by keeping yourselves pure and blameless before the Lord. Do not let the enemy, your carnal friends, or family members tell you to test the waters or to test drive the car before you buy it.

You better seek the Lord and make sure it's the right person you're going to marry, then MARRY her, men! Do not have sex with her, because your girlfriend or betrothed is someone's daughter and sister. Treat her with the same respect you would want your daughter or sister to be treated with. Women, don't lay down with a man until he marries you! Make sure he makes it clear to you what his intent is for your relationship before you agree to a courtship with him! There is absolutely NO NEED to waste time emotionally, mentally, financially, spiritually, and physically with someone who God has not revealed to be your spouse.

I'M GLAD I WAITED

I waited fourteen years for God to fulfill His promise to me for marriage. During that time period, I went through a myriad of emotions. I have seen many people get married before me. I was a groomsman in a few of my friends' weddings, even down to the month before I got married. Yes, it was disheartening to see my friends and others on social media get married while I was stuck being single and serving the Lord.

You may think I'm crazy for that last sentence you just read, but truth be told: I wanted to be married simply because God said I would. Secondly, and let's be real, I wanted to have sex. Thirdly, I wanted to have a family. After I got married, I was asked, "How does it feel to be married?" I answered: "It feels right." God gave me the desires of my heart, which also happened to be a part of His will for my life. God desires marriage. He does not want you sharing your seed or body with different men and women just because they appear desirable. He wants you to be married to one person, of the opposite sex, for the rest of your life. A marriage is meant to mirror the relationship between Christ and the church, His bride (Ephesians 5:23-27).

I am glad I waited so that Trina and I could display the

Gospel through our marriage, and moreover to share a life together and to love the way God says we should love. I have always sought to live my life according to what the Word says. Living according to the Bible is the only Way I want to live. It's the only way that makes sense to me. If I wanted to have sex, then I had to get married in order to do so. More importantly, sharing a life with someone, building that life together, having children and raising a family, for me, can only be done through marriage because it's what pleases God. Having children out of wedlock was not something I wanted to do, and having sex before marriage doesn't please the Father, so I chose marriage. Marriage is a beautiful thing because it is ordained by God. Sex is also a beautiful thing, when it happens within marriage.

Now just because you get married, does not mean your life will be void of sexual temptation. The enemy will try to destroy your marriage. He will try to send men and women to break up your marriage through adultery. The devil will try to make you think crazy thoughts to not want to stay married, but you have to cast those thoughts down when they try to exalt themselves above the knowledge of God and make them obedient to Christ! Cast down those thoughts, and go back to what brought you and your spouse together and why God brought you together.

I'm glad I waited, because it showed God's faithfulness. God was faithful to fulfill His promise to me. And that fulfillment has strengthened my faith in God tremendously. It makes me believe that God will do everything He says He will do, without doubt clouding my thoughts. If you wait on God, He will renew your strength to keep fighting against sexual immorality. He will give you the strength during those weak moments to turn away from the fine dime that just walked by, young man. He will give you the strength to not give in to your ex again daughter of God.

Be willing to say no to your flesh and yes to living the way the Bible says you should live. It will be challenging but you can do ALL THINGS through Christ Jesus who strengthens you. Just believe that you can, and then walk in your freedom!

Allow Christ to live victoriously through you by saying no to your flesh. No to sex. No to pornography. No to masturbation. No to homosexuality. No to prostitution and no to any other sexual thing that the enemy is trying to tempt you with. You do not have to let these sins reign in your body (Romans 6:12). You have the power to not obey its lusts. You can make it to marriage and even heaven without having sex. How, you may ask. Well, because Jesus did!

> *I can do ALL THINGS through Christ who strengthens me.*
>
> —Philippians 4:13

Believe that Scripture, and walk it out with God holding your hand every step of the way. Reach out to your pastor and church leaders, along with brothers and sisters of the Faith to help hold you accountable. Ask the Holy Spirit to remind you daily of Scriptures that will help keep you from sexual immorality. Keep pushing against those sexual impulses and desires. Ask the Holy Spirit to give you the strength to overcome sexual immorality. Even if you mess up and sin against God in this manner or otherwise, YOU ARE FORGIVEN! For the Scriptures declare:

> *If we confess our sins, He is faithful and just to forgive us our sins and to cleanse us from all unrighteousness.*
> —1 John 1:9

I truly hope and pray that this book has been a blessing to you. I pray that the Scriptures I've outlined throughout these pages, along with my story, help you. I pray that everything that the Holy Spirit has written through me to you will help you overcome sexual immorality so you can live life victoriously over all things sexually sinful to God. I pray that you counter the culture by living like Jesus did. Remember to love God with your body. Your body is valuable to Him, so it should be valuable to you. Save sex for your spouse and do it within the beautiful confines of marriage. You have the victory through Christ over sin, so live that victory out and walk in your freedom today! Live. Love. REIGN!

 # SOURCES

Apollo Apps LLC. G.O.P. God Over Porn. "Apollo Apps LLC, Version 1.3, 2018. apolloappdesign.com

Faks, Ibrahim. Blockade - Block Porn & Ads. "Sally Foks, Version 2.0.1, 2020. http://blockadeapp.com/termas.html

Merriam-Webster, Inc. Merriam-Webster Dictionary App. Merriam-Webster, Inc., 2021. Version 5.5.2. merriam-webster.com

Strong, James. Strong's Exhaustive Concordance of the Bible. Peabody, Massachusetts, Hendrickson Publishers, Inc., 2007.

CPSIA information can be obtained
at www.ICGtesting.com
Printed in the USA
BVHW060959181121
621927BV00009B/497